BLAKE

# BLAKE

## by ALAN CLUTTON-BROCK

### Great Lives

**HASKELL HOUSE PUBLISHERS** Ltd.
*Publishers of Scarce Scholarly Books*
**NEW YORK, N. Y. 10012**
1970

First Published 1933


**HASKELL HOUSE PUBLISHERS** Ltd.
*Publishers of Scarce Scholarly Books*
280 LAFAYETTE STREET
NEW YORK, N. Y. 10012




Library of Congress Catalog Card Number: **77-119438**




Standard Book Number 8383-1055-9

# CONTENTS

*Chapter* I      .      .      .      .      9

Blake's birth – his family – his childhood and education as an artist – early opinions on art – his marriage – Catherine Blake.

*Chapter* II      .      .      .      .      27

Blake's literary friends – the *Poetical Sketches* – *An
Island in the Moon* – his discovery of a new method of
illumination – the *Songs of Innocence and of Experience*.

*Chapter* III      .      .      .      .      52

Blake's mysticism and philosophy – *The Marriage
of Heaven and Hell* – *Visions of the Daughters of
Albion* – his revolutionary friends – he rescues an
ill-treated boy – his personal appearance – Sir
Joshua Reynolds – removal to Lambeth – Thomas
Butts – his work as an engraver and treatment of
his patrons.

*Chapter* IV      .      .      .      .      73

The prophetic books – Blake's archæological and
other theories – his insanity – criticism of his painting and engraving.

*Chapter* V      .      .      .      .      101

Blake's three years at Felpham – William Hayley
– trial for treason – discontent – return to London
– Malkin's memoir of his son – quarrel with Cromek
– epigrams on Hayley – the exhibition of 1809.

*Chapter* VI      .      .      .      .      123

Years of neglect – " The Everlasting Gospel " –
- lost works – friendship with Linnell – conversations
with Crabb Robinson – *The Ancients* – Blake's death.

# CHRONOLOGY

1757....Birth of William Blake.

1767....Blake went to Pars' drawing school.

1769....Earliest poems known.

1771....Blake apprenticed to an engraver.

1778....End of apprenticeship. Studied in the Royal Academy schools.

1782....Blake married Catherine Boucher.

1783....*Poetical Sketches* privately printed.

1787....Possible date of *An Island in the Moon*.

1789....*Songs of Innocence* and *The Book of Thel*.

1791....*The French Revolution* printed. Blake made friends with revolutionary philosophers.

1792....Removal to Lambeth.

1793....Probable date of *The Marriage of Heaven and Hell*. *Visions of the Daughters of Albion*.

1794....*The Songs of Experience* engraved. *The Book of Urizen*.

1800....Blake went to Felpham.

1804....Blake returned to London.

1809....Exhibition of Blake's pictures.

1818....*Jerusalem* probably finished.
　　　　Blake made the acquaintance of John
　　　　Linnell.
1825....Engravings of the Book of Job.
　　　　Conversations with Crabb Robinson.
1827....Designs and engravings to illustrate
　　　　Dante. Blake's death.

# CHAPTER I

Blake's birth – his family – his childhood and education as an artist – early opinions on art – his marriage – Catherine Blake.

IT has often been said that William Blake, being born in the middle of the eighteenth century, was born out of his time. But it is hard to think of any state of civilisation in which he would have been more comfortable. He lived within the recesses of his mind, and his contacts with the outside world were often oblique and disconcerting. His mind was more real to him than anything outside it ; it was to its promptings that he deferred ; to his own voice, and to no other, that he listened. It is true that in earlier times he might have been elected a saint, but he would more probably have been burnt for a heretic, as, indeed, were some of his works, by his Roman Catholic admirer, Frederick Tatham. At a later date he might have had many more readers, and even founded a mystical sect, but he would more probably have been locked up for a lunatic. It was much safer to hear voices, converse with angels, and reconstruct the universe before the democratic State had learnt to exercise its efficient supervision. And,

if he had escaped certification, is it to be supposed
that he would have found our own time, or any
time in the last century, a congenial period ?
D. H. Lawrence, who had some affinity with
Blake, though he was much more concerned with
the world outside his own mind, was not satisfied
with the twentieth century. Blake might con-
ceivably have been more prosperous to-day, but
it is unlikely that even the combined efforts of
all his modern admirers would have served to put
him at his ease. At any time, it may be supposed,
he would have been able to write :

> *The Angel that presided o'er my birth*
> *Said, " Little creature, form'd of Joy & Mirth,*
> *" Go love without the help of any Thing on Earth."*

He was born on November 28th, 1757, in Soho,
the son of a fairly prosperous hosier. Students of
heredity might observe that his father, though
often only referred to as a Dissenter, was sometimes called a Swedenborgian, and that his elder
brother, James – although, as Tatham tells us,
" having a saving, somniferous mind, he lived a
yard-and-a-half life and pestered his brother
with timid sentences of bread and cheese advice "
– was nevertheless thought a little mad by his
neighbours because he would " talk Swedenborg."

His brother John – " my brother John, the evil
one " – enlisted in the army, lived wildly, and
died young. Robert, Blake's favourite brother,
learnt engraving from William, and lived with
him for three years, but died at an early age.
A curious drawing by Robert may be seen in the
print-room of the British Museum, and it would
be tempting to advance the theory that Robert
was really the greater artist of the two. But
though this drawing has a curiously modern air –
it might almost be an imitation of an early
Matisse – it is hardly enough by itself to support
such a theory. No other member of the family
seems to have been remarkable either for
talent or eccentricity, and nothing is known of
Blake's mother or of any earlier generation of
Blakes.

William Blake was an interesting and what
would now be called a difficult child. His father
found that he resented any beating or correction
so severely that he could not send him to school.
One would not have expected a Dissenting
hosier to have much patience either with
oddity or with artistic inclinations, but Blake
seems to have been educated in a manner that
would only be allowed by the most enlightened
parents of to-day. He was encouraged to learn
drawing from his earliest years and had little

other teaching, with the curious result that he
became a poet and later learnt several living and
dead languages. But his father was not so in-
dulgent to his habit of seeing and describing
visions. Apparently he was not corrected for
seeing God for the first, but by no means for the
last time, at the age of four, when God " put
His head to the window " and made him scream
with fright. But when, at about the age of eight,
he returned from a walk to say that at Peckham
Rye he had seen a tree filled with angels, his
father would have beaten him for telling a lie if
his mother had not protected him, and he did
not escape when later he saw Ezekiel. It seems
to be agreed by most critics that Blake's father
later became to him a symbol for every kind of
hateful authority, or, rather, that every kind of
hateful authority became a symbol for his father.
In various versions of his poems he alters the
words father, serpent, and priest as though they
were interchangeable synonyms. The only rational
grounds – although of course it is unnecessary
to look for any rational grounds – for Blake's
identification of his father with oppression and
authority is that his father discouraged his
visions. In everything else, what little we know
of him suggests that he was a model parent of a
neurotic child.

But these visions must have seemed of trans-
cendent importance to the infant Blake. It is
curious to notice how like in content and flavour
they are to his later poems. His vision, during
another walk in the beautiful suburbs of eighteenth-century London, of angels walking among
the haymakers in a field, might easily be the
subject of one of the *Songs of Innocence*. Beauty
was always to him of this visionary kind, but he
never had to go far afield to find it. Any occasion,
a service, for example, of charity school children
in St. Paul's, could be as easily transfigured into
a supernatural event as the incidents of these
childish walks.

At the age of ten Blake was sent to Pars'
drawing school in the Strand, where he was
taught to draw from casts of antique sculpture,
but not from the living model. He had studied
pictures and prints even before this time, and
was sent to school because he already showed a
passion for drawing. His father also bought him
casts from which he could work at home and gave
him pocket-money with which to buy prints.
And even at this early age, Blake had formed his
taste. He despised the works of the Seicento,
which were fashionable at the time, and confined
his attention to the painters of the High Renaissance. His youthful companions at the school,

not recognising how much in advance of the fashion Blake was, used to laugh at his " mechanical taste." But " I am happy," Blake wrote in later life ; " I cannot say that Raffaelle ever was from my earliest childhood hidden from me. I saw and I knew immediately the difference between Raffaelle and Rubens."

As a matter of fact, Raphael must have been almost impenetrably hidden from him. He can have seen few if any of his original works, since he never left England and there was then no National Gallery. He himself admitted that he had never seen any original works by his other favourite, Michelangelo, but then he was assured by the Archangel Gabriel that Michelangelo could draw angels, and that the Archangel was in a position to know, because he had sat to Michelangelo. But, apart from such supernatural sources of information, Blake could only have seen engravings and perhaps a few doubtful drawings. There exists an early engraving by him with the inscription " Michael Angelo *pinxit* " and the title " Joseph of Arimathea among the Rocks of Albion " – not a very likely title for a Michelangelo though a very probable one for a Blake—and the derivation from Michelangelo, though recognisable, is remote. From their engravings, which he also admired and collected, he would have gained a more

direct acquaintance with the works of Dürer
and the German school.

It was, it would seem, the clear definition of
every form by an undisturbed outline – the
linear style, as it is sometimes called – which he
chiefly admired in the painters of the High
Renaissance, qualities which would be even more
obvious in engravings from their works than in the
originals.   He hated the obliteration of outline
either by colour laid on with a full brush – he had
a violent hatred of the paint-brush – or by the
use of chiaroscuro.   In time the matter came to
assume an almost cosmic importance, and Newton, a worse bogey even than the paint-brush, was
dragged into the dispute.    With deliberate
sarcasm he wrote :

> *That God is Colouring Newton does shew,*
> *And the devil is a Black outline, all of us know.*

The Venetian painters, he observed, were guilty of
obliterating the outline, and so :

> *Venetian, all thy Colouring is no more*
> *Than Boulster'd Plasters on a Crooked Whore.*

And, because Poussin's outlines are clear while
Rembrandt's are not, he hazarded the extraordinary statement, which is surely the exact

reverse of the truth, that " Rembrandt was a Generalizer. Poussin was a Particularizer."

It would be a simple explanation of Blake's opinions that he only admired those works which bore some resemblance to his own style. But this hardly explains why he first took up with this style, or why at so tender an age his opinions were already secure. One may find some explanation in Blake's infallible instinct for the primitive, since at this time the artists of the High Renaissance occupied almost the same position as the primitives in the nineteenth century. But, even so, it is hardly possible to doubt that there was some mysterious psychological process at work, more urgent than the usual preferences of normal artists in matters of style, which made him prefer outline from his earliest years and later attribute to it a moral and mystical significance. In one of his most cryptic and mystical works about the ultimate nature of the universe, *The Ghost of Abel*, he writes : " Nature has no Outline, but Imagination has. Nature has no Tune, but Imagination has. Nature has no Supernatural & dissolves : Imagination is Eternity." And this gives us, I think, a clue to what outline meant to Blake. In painting it performed the same function as imagination, in Blake's particular sense of the word, in poetry. Just as in his prophetic books Blake, by the use of imagination, could create an imaginary universe which was far more satisfactory to him than the dissolving and painful chaos of nature, so in painting only those objects which were carefully outlined seemed to him to partake of the same imaginary, artificial, and complete character. In fact, they, and they alone, belonged to the fantastic world which he created for himself as a refuge from the painful aspects of reality. But objects represented by chiaroscuro belonged to the real world, as he makes quite clear in the poem quoted above, in which Newton, as a materialist and a scientist, is made responsible for colour. In the same poem he describes a dog swimming with a bone in its mouth –

*As he swam he saw the reflection of the bone.*
*" This is quite Perfection, one Generalizing Tone !*
*" Outline ! There's no outline ! There's no such*
*thing !*
*" All is Chiaro Scuro, Poco Pen, it's all colouring."*
*Snap, Snap ! he has lost shadow & substance too.*
*He had them before ; now how do ye do ?*

In other words, whatever was represented by chiaroscuro and colour belonged to the illusory and temporary world of sensation. For, of course,

Bb

Blake believed that his artificial universe was far more real than Nature, or the vegetable universe as he sometimes called it. Outline was a method of abstraction, and so Blake paradoxically endowed it with the attributes of reality. This matter of outline may seem a small matter on which to dwell, but it is the chief indication that even in his childhood he looked to works of art to provide him with a refuge from reality, and passionately resented anything which brought them nearer, as chiaroscuro and colour undoubtedly do, to an imitation of the sensible world. In fact, it was more true than he thought when he said that " Madmen see outlines & therefore they draw them."

It is possible that it was his love of outline which inclined Blake towards engraving. There was some talk of apprenticing him to an eminent painter, for which a very large premium was needed. Since even to a family of such moderate means the position of a painter must then have seemed extremely precarious, this again argues great magnanimity in Blake's parents. Perhaps Blake was already afraid of the paint-brush, but this hardly detracts from his equal magnanimity in refusing the offer because it would not have been fair to take so much money from his brothers and sisters. He decided instead to work with an

engraver, which would cost much less. His father
took him to the studio of a certain Ryland, but
Blake refused to have anything to do with him.
" I do not like the man's face," he explained ;
" it looks as if he will live to be hanged." Twelve
years later Ryland was hanged for forgery.
Blake made several other successful prophecies
during his life, but he also made a good many
which were unsuccessful. He was apprenticed,
at a cost of fifty guineas, to Basire, a sound, old-
fashioned engraver who was employed by learned
societies to illustrate antiquities – here again
Blake encountered the primitive – and had made
the largest engraving yet attempted by anyone, a
reproduction of a picture of the Field of the Cloth
of Gold in the King's collection. After two years'
engraving, Blake quarrelled so much with his
fellow-apprentices " concerning matters of intellectual argument " – he had already, one may
suppose, begun to advance theories about the
nature of the universe – that he was sent out to
make drawings of Gothic monuments, chiefly in
Westminster Abbey. In this occupation, which
he evidently enjoyed, he spent five years, and in
Westminster Abbey had another vision, this time
of Christ and the Apostles. But he appears to
have found some opportunities for quarrelling
even in the Abbey, where the Westminster

schoolboys were then allowed to play. They set
themselves to tease Blake, and one of them
climbed on the scaffolding where he was drawing
a monument, which so much enraged Blake that
he threw him to the floor. He might very easily,
one would think, have found himself in trouble
for this, but he actually succeeded, by a complaint
to the Dean, in having the schoolboys turned
out of the Abbey for good.

Blake was moved to the greatest enthusiasm by
the Gothic sculptures which he had to draw, the
most primitive objects which he had yet encountered. At the top of the same engraving of Joseph
of Arimathea mentioned above, executed when
he was sixteen, he wrote :

" This is One of the Gothic Artists who Built
the Cathedrals in what we call the Dark Ages,
Wandering about in sheep skins & goat skins, of
whom the World was not worthy ; such were the
Christians in all Ages."

Did Blake mean that Joseph of Arimathea actually
built cathedrals, or is this only an alternative
title to the engraving ? It is hard to say, but in
any case he was capable of equally remarkable
adventures in the history of art. " What we call
Antique Gems," he later decided, " are the Gems

of Aaron's breastplate." It is interesting to see
how completely Blake anticipated the theory
of Ruskin and the Pre-Raphaelites that primitive
artists were exceptionally virtuous characters.

During his seven years' apprenticeship Blake
was not only working at his trade with that energy
which he always applied to all his activities ; he
also wrote some of the poems which later appeared in the *Poetical Sketches*. But, since this
book was not printed till 1783, it may well be left
till we come to that time. After his apprenticeship he studied for a short time in the Antique
School of the Royal Academy under Moser, a
teacher who was thought well of at the time.
Blake did not admire him. He records that Moser
reproved him for studying prints from Raphael
and Michelangelo. "You should not," said
Moser, "study these old, hard, stiff, and dry,
unfinished works of art," and he recommended
Rubens and Le Brun as models. Blake, of
course, was furious ; he had been touched on the
raw, and "How did I secretly rage," he says.
But he also objected to drawing from the life,
although he did on occasion do so, and a com-
petent but dull drawing of a nude young man still
exists which was obviously taken from a living
model, perhaps from his brother Robert. Blake
thought drawing from life more like death, and

that it "smelt of mortality." Here again we find
him hating everything but the artificial constructions of his mind. and moved by a violent and
neurotic revulsion from reality as it appeared to
his ordinary senses. Yet a large water-colour
drawing in the historical style, painted about this
time and representing " The Penance of Jane
Shore," has hardly a trace of that visionary
quality which marks his later works, and in
another work of the same time, representing
" The Ordeal of Queen Emma," there is little
beyond a stiff, classical, and sterile elegance.
Nevertheless, Blake must have seen something
which we can hardly see in these pictures, for he
included the former in his exhibition of 1809,
with which he intended to establish his reputation,
and in the catalogue remarks that the picture
" proves to the Author, and he thinks will prove
to any discerning eye, that the productions of
our youth and of our mature years are equal in
all respects." At this time Blake was employed
by the booksellers, and made many engravings, mostly after the designs of other artists.
Occasionally he had even to do fashion-plates.
But he got to know several artists of reputation,
among whom were Stothard and Flaxman, and
in the year 1780 he had a water-colour of " The
Death of Earl Godwin " in the Royal Academy.

In his twenty-fourth year Blake was much troubled by love for a " lively little girl " called Polly Wood. He himself said that she was " no trifler," but she seems in fact to have trifled with his affections, for she allowed him her company without any thought of marrying him. He complained that she went about with other young men, but she only asked him, " Are you a fool ? " " That," Blake says, " cured me of jealousy " ; but, as it happens, he was made so ill that he was sent for a change of air to the house of a market-gardener in Battersea, Boucher or Boutcher by name. There he related his sorrow to the daughter of the house, Catherine Boucher, who expressed her sympathy. He immediately asked, " Do you pity me ? " and when she answered, " Yes, indeed I do," he said, " Then I love you " ; and that, it appears, was all their courtship. But Catherine had already fallen in love with him. When she first saw him she knew at once that he would be her future husband, and was " so near fainting that she had to leave the room." Blake returned to his lodgings in London and there worked incessantly for about a year, resolving not to see Catherine until he had made enough money for them to marry. When he had done so, they were married in Battersea Church in August 1782.

Blake may not have been perfectly happy with
his wife, but it is hardly likely that he would have
been perfectly happy with anyone. He seems at
times to have had a clear and conscious desire for
polygamy ; he even recommended community
of wives, and talked of bringing a concubine into
the house. His prophetic books, in which, to
use his own words, he was occupied with " weaving to dreams the sexual strife," show that he was
much troubled with such notions and such desires.
Whether he ever put them into practice it is, of
course, impossible to say. But Catherine seems
to have been the most patient and devoted of
wives. She was a good housekeeper, very
punctual and precise, and even when she could
have afforded a servant she preferred to do all the
work herself. She looked after her improvident
husband in all his troubles and, it is said, always
kept a guinea hidden away which was not to be
used except in the last necessity. Blake himself
could hardly bear even to speak of money, and
violently protested when the subject was mentioned to him. Mrs. Blake had to devise the
plan of putting before him whatever food was in
the house, without saying a word, and when he
saw before him an empty plate he knew that he
must bestir himself. But she combined her
practical and determined common sense with a

complete and entire belief in everything that her
husband said.  She never doubted that he saw
visions, and she accepted all his ideas as a divine
revelation of the truth.  When he would tell a
friend that some visionary being had sat for him,
she would look at her husband with awe, and then
turn to the listener to confirm the fact.  Indeed,
she herself in time came to see visions, and also
learnt to draw in a manner very like her husband's.  An observer of them in their old age
noted that she " partook of his insanity," but
she seems to have accepted quietly and without
conflict, as an unreflecting mind accepts its
religion, those beliefs to which Blake himself was
forced by intense emotional disturbances.  She
was an uneducated woman whom Blake had to
teach to read and write, and no doubt he always
had a complete intellectual ascendancy over her.
She always addressed him as Mr. Blake, and he her
as Kate.  She would go with him into the country
on walks that took all day and some of the night,
and when Blake woke in the middle of the night
and was driven to write at a feverish speed what
his spirits dictated to him, she too would wake
and sit silently by his side to soothe him.  It is
no wonder that, however much in his youth he
was troubled with sexual longings, or, what is
much the same thing, by sexual theories, and

however much she may have shown her jealousy, he never ceased to love her. In her youth she was beautiful and dark ; in her old age she is said to have grown coarse in appearance except, as an observer noted, " in so far as love made her otherwise, and spoke through her gleaming black eyes." They had no children.

# CHAPTER II

Blake's literary friends – the *Poetical Sketches* – *An Island in the Moon* – his discovery of a new method of illumination – the *Songs of Innocence and of Experience.*

AFTER his marriage Blake was first introduced to the literary world, or, rather, to a mild and unimportant section of it – a group of literary and artistic persons, chiefly blue-stocking ladies, who used to meet in the drawing-room of " the accomplished Mrs. Mathew," the wife of a clergyman who enjoyed the reputation of reading the service more beautifully than any other clergyman in London. But even here Blake was able to indulge his taste for eccentric company, towards which, as one can infer, he was irresistibly attracted. Thomas Taylor, the Platonist, from whom Blake derived his acquaintance with Greek philosophy, was one of the company. Platonism may seem an innocent, even a mild, occupation, but Taylor, whether in pursuit of his studies or for some other reason, tried to invent a perpetual lamp, and actually succeeded in burning down the Freemason's Tavern. What is more to the point, and must have been pleasant to Blake, Taylor believed firmly in all the mythology of Olympus, and a Frenchman, with the agility of his race, succeeded in making love to Taylor's wife by pretending that he was worshipping Aphrodite. The Mathews discovered and encouraged the sculptor Flaxman, who in return decorated their drawing-room with " models in putty and sand, of figures in niches in the Gothic manner." The windows were painted in imitation of stained glass and the " book-cases, tables and chairs were ornamented to accord with the appearance of those of anti-quity." In this congenial interior Blake would sing his poems to tunes of his own which were taken down by " professional musicians." And Mr. Mathew was so much impressed with his verses that he undertook the printing of them in a small volume, which came out in 1783 and appears to have been noticed by very few outside the circle, although in course of time the *literati* paid some attention to it. Mr. Mathew contributed a preface in which he apologised for the irregularities and faults of the verses, which he wished to excuse by the poet's defective education, and remarked that Blake had been too busy to correct the proofs. These were the poems which Blake had begun to write in his twelfth year. The poem beginning " How sweet I roamed from field to field . . . " was written before he was fourteen.

It was a miraculous precocity, for among
these poems are perhaps the most perfect lyrics
of the eighteenth century. It is true that few of
them are properly of the eighteenth century and
the most famous of them, the poem " To the
Muses," beginning " Whether on Ida's shady
brow . . . " is a lament for the decline of poetry
at that time. But, whatever style he chose to
imitate, Blake was always capable of an astonishing originality, and in the few poems of this
collection in which he uses the conventions of
eighteenth-century verse his gifts are still instantly apparent. There is an urgency of feeling
which at once converts these stock phrases of
poetic diction into something entirely different,
which strips them of their trite associations and
gives them that new and pungent flavour which
seems to be an essential quality of the diction of
real poetry.

> *Our bards are fam'd who strike the silver wire :*
> *Our youths are bolder than the southern swains :*
> *Our maidens fairer in the sprightly dance ;*
> *We lack not songs, nor instruments of joy,*
> *Nor echoes sweet, nor waters clear as heaven,*
> *Nor laurel wreaths against the sultry heat.*

Here no doubt it is chiefly the rhythm – for Blake
could always make his rhythms sound with a

purely individual accent – which changes the
" silver wire," the " swains," the " echoes sweet,"
and the " laurel wreaths " into poetry, but it is
probable that something more has happened to
invest these familiar symbols in their context with
a richer, a more significant burden of association.
Even so, Blake is always breaking away from such
symbols, into the world of his own imagination,
in which only his own individual images can
exist.  Thus, after such conventional, literary lines
as these :

> *With sweet May dews my wings were wet,*
> *And Phœbus fir'd my vocal rage . . .*

he immediately passes into his own individual
poetic territory :

> *He caught me in his silken net,*
> *And shut me in his golden cage.*

> *He loves to sit and hear me sing,*
> *Then, laughing, sports and plays with me ;*
> *Then stretches out my golden wing,*
> *And mocks my loss of liberty.*

Here he speaks almost as later in the *Songs of
Innocence,* and yet this is the particular poem which
is said to have been written before he was fourteen.

But it is clear from these early poems that he had not once for all found his own subjects or style. He sought among the poems of the past, and chiefly among the Elizabethans, for a kind of poetry which should suit him better than that of his immediate predecessors or of his contemporaries. The song "My silks and fine array" might almost be an Elizabethan poem, and it is one of the few existing examples of an exact imitation of a much earlier style of poetry which has no academic or archaistic flavour. But I suppose that if one came across it for the first time without knowing its author, one might guess that it was by Blake. And though the song "Love and harmony combine" obviously has some relation to Shakespeare's "The Phœnix and the Turtle," after a few lines it moves into a rhythm and a diction entirely individual to Blake and very characteristic of his later poems.

> *Thou the golden fruit dost bear,*
> *I am clad in flowers fair ;*
> *Thy sweet boughs perfume the air,*
> *And the turtle buildeth there.*
>
> *There she sits and feeds her young,*
> *Sweet I hear her mournful song ;*
> *And thy lovely leaves among,*
> *There is love ; I hear his tongue.*

In the same volume there is also an imitation –
not a very good imitation – of Spenser, a ballad
of a Gothic and violent character, and a long
fragment of a play about King Edward III and
the battle of Crécy. Although this is superficially
a tolerably exact imitation of Shakespeare's
historical plays, but without any dramatic
qualities whatever, a closer inspection almost
suggests that Blake has attempted in this incon-
gruous form the first of his prophetic books. There
is already an apocalyptic fervour in his patriotism
of a kind which continually reappears in his later
works. And the English soldiers in France speak
as though they were on the eve of the millennium
instead of on the eve of the battle of Crécy.
Albion is already almost the New Jerusalem :

*I'll fight and weep, 'tis in my country's cause ;*
*I'll weep and shout for glorious liberty.*
*Grim war shall laugh and shout, decked in tears,*
*And blood shall flow like streams across the meadows,*
*That murmur down their pebbly channels, and*
*Spend their sweet lives to do their country service :*
*Then shall England's verdure shoot, her fields shall smile,*
*Her ships shall sing across the foaming sea,*
*Her mariners shall use the flute and viol,*
*And rattling guns, and black and dreary war,*
*Shall be no more.*

This is not only a war to end wars, but to bring in
the earthly paradise. And the play ends with a
minstrel's song in which there appear, by no means
for the last time, the giant and godlike ancestors
of the English. For Blake was inclined to find
supernatural virtues in the past as well as in the
future, preferably in a past about which very little
is known, just as D. H. Lawrence found perfect
virtue only amongst the Etruscans. And here
these " enormous sons of Ocean " prophesy the
greatness of the English.

*Their mighty wings shall stretch from east to west,*
*Their nest is in the sea ; but they shall roam*
*Like eagles for their prey ; nor shall the young*
*Crave or be heard ; plenty shall bring forth,*
*Cities shall sing, and vales in rich array*
*Shall laugh, whose fruitful laps bend down with fulness.*

Here also Blake inclined to the theory that the
English are descended from the Trojan Brutus, as
later he was to believe that they are the ten lost
tribes. And in yet another war song, which
probably belongs to the same time and mood
as the play, the personages of English history are
suspiciously like the symbolical figures of Blake's
subsequent mythology.

*Alfred shall smile, and make his harp rejoice ;*
*The Norman William, and the learned Clerk,*
Cʙ

> *And Lion Heart, and black-brow'd Edward with*
> *His loyal queen shall rise, and welcome us !*

At this moment, in his early youth, Blake seems
to be constructing his imaginary universe out of
the history of England, whose personages have
now come out of the past into that vague and
undated future when every wish will be fulfilled.
And it is a curious fact that already, when he is
most obviously engaged in writing an apocalypse,
he loses the precision of poetry and grows vague
and diffuse.

But as yet he had by no means developed his full
philosophy of life.  For in this volume he derives
from a story of cheating at Blind Man's Buff the
moral that :

> *. . . those who play should stop the same*
> *By wholesome laws, such as – all those*
> *Who on the blinded man impose*
> *Stand in his stead ; as, long a-gone,*
> *When men were first a nation grown,*
> *Lawless they liv'd—till wantonness*
> *And liberty began t'increase,*
> *And one man lay in another's way ;*
> *Then laws were made to keep fair play.*

Such sentiments Blake would afterwards have
indignantly repudiated, if, indeed, he could have

been persuaded to listen to them at all. For, alas, they are a most cogent and destructive criticism of his whole system of ethics.

In the year after the publication of these poems Blake was still intimate with the Mathews and their circle, for it is in this year that he is reported to have set his poems to music and to have sung them to the company. But shortly afterwards, " in consequence," we are told, " of his unbending deportment, or what his adherents are pleased to call manly firmness of opinion, which certainly was not at all times considered pleasing by everyone," his visits grew less frequent. Obviously Blake was not suited for a *salon*, although at a much later date, when his opinions had grown even more firm, he went to a party given by Lady Caroline Lamb, where Lady Charlotte Bury thought him " full of beautiful imaginations and genius." But, even then, Lady Charlotte could not help being amused at the strange manner in which Lady Caroline had made up her party, while Sir Thomas Lawrence, even though he is known to have had a great admiration for Blake's pictures, appears to have been most careful to keep his distance.

In the year of his departure from the *salon*, or possibly rather later, Blake wrote an extravagant

sketch of the company, which is unfinished and
was probably never intended to be published.
*An Island in the Moon,* as its romantic title suggests,
is to some extent another attempt to find a literary
form for an artificial universe. Mr. Symons
remarks that it shows us " Blake's first wholly
irresponsible attempt to create imaginary worlds
and to invent grotesque and impossible names."
But, as I have said, I should be inclined to call
*Edward III* Blake's first essay in artificial universes,
and there is a first faint trace of odd names in a
romantic ballad on the subject of Gwin of Norway
which also appears in the *Poetical Sketches.* Nevertheless in *An Island in the Moon* Blake plays with
words and invents names in a far more curious
and striking manner and with an almost hysterical
profusion of eccentric syllables. But, being a satire,
this imaginary world is still incompletely free
from reality. As Blake himself puts it, the island
" seems to have some affinity to England," but
when he continues " . . . the people are so much
alike, & their language so much the same, that
you would think you was among your friends,"
he goes too far. Although, as has often been observed, it has a faint flavour of Peacock, it is a
purely fantastic burlesque, approaching nearer
to *surréalisme* than to accurate satire. As a document of his mind it is of some importance. For

here his bogey, Newton, makes his first appearance, and he first displays his hatred of science
in disorderly and strident ridicule. Thus surgery,
the child of " old corruption " :

> . . . *form'd a crooked knife,*
> *And ran about with bloody hands*
> *To seek his mother's life.*

There are some very amusing songs in the course
of the narrative, but, what is more extraordinary,
in the midst of the turmoil, the angry and agitated
burlesque, in the mouths of the absurd mathe-
matician Mr. Obtuse Angel, of the farcical Mrs.
Nannicantipot, and of Quid the Cynic, there
are put three of the *Songs of Innocence* in a first
version. It is a sudden flowering in the desert,
and nothing more clearly shows how opposed were
the two courses which Blake's troubled mind
could take. He could write poetry or he could
spin out fantastic nonsense, but seldom anything
between the two.

When Blake's father died, in 1784, he set up a
print-shop with a fellow-apprentice next door to
his father's old house in Soho. His favourite
brother, Robert, came to live with them and to
learn engraving. But Robert died within three
years and Blake soon gave up the print-shop,

which had not been very successful. When
Robert was dead and Blake had seen his soul rise
through the ceiling "clapping his hands for
joy," he slept for three days and nights, and ever
afterwards he saw Robert "in my remembrance,
in the regions of my imagination." "Even now,"
he wrote, thirteen years after his brother's
death, "I hear his advice and write from his
dictate." And it was the spirit of Robert who
suggested to Blake a new method of "illuminated
printing," a process which was the exact opposite
of etching. The lines to be printed from the
copper-plate were drawn in varnish or some
material impervious to acid and the surrounding
exposed area of the plate bitten away to the
required depth. It was this process which he
used in printing all his subsequent books. As a
matter of fact, his friend Cumberland, who some
years before was at work on a rather similar
process, may have suggested it to Blake. And in
*An Island in the Moon* there is a reference to this
method, which, it is clear, Blake thought would
make his fortune. Someone is speaking of a
method of "illuminating the manuscript."

"'Then,' said he, 'I would have all the writing
Engraved instead of Printed, & at every other
leaf a high finish'd print – all in three Volumes

folio – & sell them a hundred pounds apiece.
They would print off two thousand.'

" ' Then,' said she, ' whoever will not have
them will be ignorant fools & will not deserve
to live.' "

Blake did not make as much as two hundred
thousand pounds from his invention.   Unfortunately, it is impossible to know for certain
whether *An Island in the Moon* was written before
or after Robert's death.   If it was written before,
this would be a striking example of the way in
which visionary commands arranged themselves
in Blake's mind.   Whatever the origin of the
process, it seems to have soon assumed almost
magical properties in his mind, for in *The Marriage
of Heaven and Hell* he refers again to it as follows :

" But first the notion that man has a body
distinct from his soul is to be expunged ; this I
shall do by printing in the infernal method, by
corrosives, which in Hell are salutary and
medicinal, melting apparent surfaces away, and
displaying the infinite which was hid."

It has been argued that this is little more than
a joke, no doubt because, if one is to suppose
that it is meant seriously, one may also be led to

suppose that his other mystical notions are equally ridiculous. It is possible that there is a certain apologetic frivolity as if to excuse the extravagance of Blake's fancy. But there is the same slight veil of humour over many of the more important ideas in *The Marriage of Heaven and Hell*. To make a joke is often a convenient method of averting ridicule, but it does not follow that Blake himself thought his ideas absurd because he feared that, without the disguise of humour, others would think them so. If he attached enough importance to the process to attribute it to the suggestion of his brothers' spirit, he may well have endowed it with other supernatural attributes.

But whether or no he attached a magical significance to this mode of illuminated printing, there is no doubt that he thought it of enormous importance in the material world. Somewhat later he brought out a prospectus of books printed in this way, in which he says that he confidently expects that the poverty and obscurity which proverbially attend the labours of the artist, the poet, and the musician, will henceforth be entirely removed by his invention. " Even Milton and Shakespeare," he says, " could not publish their own works," with the obvious inference that, if they had known of his discovery, they would have been able to do so. And, in fact, we probably owe to this invention the survival of Blake's works. The process was first used experimentally in two minute tracts, *There is No Natural Religion* and *All Religions are One*, but the *Songs of Innocence* was the first important book to be produced in this manner, and the first in which he had mastered the process.

The *Songs of Innocence* are intended to go with the *Songs of Experience*, though these were not engraved till five years after, and the two together illustrate " the contrary states of the human soul." Thus there are many poems in the second collection which correspond to poems on the same subject in the first. The two books together are the most important collection of Blake's most perfect and intelligible poems. Indeed, it has required the labours of many critics to show how unintelligible some of them are.

Blake seems to have reached at this time – the years during which these poems were written – a point at which all the disturbances of his mind, his conflicting desires and fears, could be expressed and perhaps relieved in compact, apparently simple, and spontaneous poetry. It is possible, as his critics have shown, to unpack some of these songs into prophetic books, and after this

time Blake was to be chiefly occupied in doing
so. Henceforth he was only capable at rare
moments of this extraordinary synthesis and
compression of ideas which enriches the simplest
phrases. Instead of resolving his conflicts by
stating them with the detachment of the artist,
Blake was to exhaust himself in the creation
of diffuse mythologies. " Without Contraries,"
he said, " is no progression " ; but in the *Songs
of Innocence* and *Experience* he fortunately makes
no attempt to progress. The contradictions, the
ambivalences of the human mind, are freely
admitted, and there is little attempt to reconcile
them.

But in poetry, by a process as mysterious as it
is familiar, contradictions cease to conflict. It
is only when they are taken out of the self-sufficient
world of the work of art that the human mind
cannot tolerate them. When once the contradictions which disturbed him could no longer be
set within the sphere of poetry, Blake piled up
enormous prophecies, and constructed vast and
confusing mythologies in the desperate hope that
in the end some solution could be found. But it
was inevitably an endless treadmill. To reconcile
the existence of a just God with the existence of
evil, which can be interpreted psychologically as
the conflict between the limitless desires of the

human mind and the stubborn realities which it
encounters, leads to an endless repetition of
argument, as the history of religious controversy
amply illustrates. Blake was always attempting a
solution of similar problems, chiefly by denying
the existence of evil, which he was continually
forced to recognise, and the effort led him into
an endless flight from reality and a perpetual
attempt to construct a universe in which the law
of contradiction was not valid. It is as if Euclid
had had to form a geometry based on contradic-
tory axioms. But in poetry the law of contradiction is at any rate suspended. *Paradise Lost*, in
so far as it is poetry, justifies the works of God to
man ; in so far as it is argument, it notoriously
does not. And in the *Songs of Innocence* and
*Experience* the existence and the non-existence of
evil are found comfortably side by side.

Unfortunately, the resolution of contraries
which is effected in poetry is seldom lasting and
is of little use to the intellect. Thus it was inevitable that Blake should not be satisfied with
it unless he were willing to suspend all his problems, which their urgency would not allow him
to do. What actually seems to have happened is
that he tried to remain half way between poetry
and argument, or philosophy. " All sects of
philosophy," he says, " are from the Poetic

Genius adapted to the weaknesses of the individual." He saw, in fact, the likeness between
what the poet does and what the philosopher
tries to do, and he could never relinquish the
belief that poetry provides the ultimate solution,
even though he could never be content with the
particular kind of solution which poetry does
provide. He confused, in fact, the emotional
resolutions of poetry with the intellectual solutions provided by argument. And he tried to
make poetry provide the two solutions at once,
not by two completely separate functions, as in
*Paradise Lost*, but together and in one act. He
himself saw clearly where he differed from Milton,
and how distinct and separate was Milton's
argument from his poetry. " The reason Milton
wrote in fetters," he says, " when he wrote of
Angels & God, and at liberty when of Devils
& Hell, is because he was a true poet and of the
Devil's party without knowing it." He himself
could not manage such a separation because the
contraries with which he was troubled seemed so
much more urgent to him than those which Milton
so serenely evades in his simple arguments. But
if the poet must write philosophy, it is only by
some such separation that he can succeed both
in philosophising and in writing poetry. A real
mixture of the two processes is fatal ; they are

two more contraries. Thus the prophetic books
are automatically unable to produce the emotional resolutions of poetry because the writer is
being driven on by so much evident dissatisfaction
with whatever intellectual solution he can con-
trive. In fact they cannot, *ipso facto*, be poetry,
except where, as happens at rare intervals, Blake
forgets for the moment to pursue his chase and is
content with a temporary emotional satisfaction.

Nevertheless, Blake's discovery of the likeness
between philosophy and poetry is, I think, both
important and true. Even more than poetry,
philosophy is often a roundabout and painless
method of talking about the less realisable desires
of the human heart. And, ultimately, it must
connect with these desires and have at least this
foundation in reality. Thus " No man can think,
write, or speak from the heart," as Blake says,
" but he must intend truth." But he does not
seem to have noticed that this is the strongest
argument against writing philosophy. Unlike
poetry, philosophy is useless unless it is not only
true, but exactly true. And circumlocution is
not a good method of reaching the exact truth ;
it is better, for this purpose, to write not from,
but about, the heart. Nevertheless, in the process
of speaking from the heart it sometimes happens
that information is given about the heart, as if

by the way.  And this is even more likely to happen in the kind of philosophy that Blake wrote,
in which his desires are much more evident, presumably because so much more urgent, than in
closely reasoned descriptions of the ultimate
nature of reality.  Thus in the course of his philosophical and mystical works he sometimes
makes revolutionary and important discoveries in
psychology, anticipating the discoveries of the
twentieth century.  Perhaps the most important
is that to repress desire is dangerous, but there
are others which are equally startling and show
an equal insight.

The most obvious characteristic of the *Songs of
Innocence* and *Experience*, by contrast with the prophetic books, is their extreme simplicity.  It has
been suggested that they were inspired by Watts's
hymns for infant minds.  It is also possible that
Blake took the idea of writing in this simple
manner, as if for children, from the blue-stocking
ladies whom he met in the Mathews' drawing-
room.  It was then the custom for clever women
to employ themselves in a harmless and decorous
manner by writing books for children, and, in the
decoration which adorns the title-page of the
*Songs of Innocence*, a woman, perhaps a blue-
stocking, may be seen reading aloud to two
children.  There is no more difficult style of poetry

than that which looks as if it might appeal to
children, and not only because the most odious
and suspect emotions are usually supposed, perhaps with reason, to be peculiarly suitable for the
nursery.    Simplicity of this kind presents innumerable problems of style which only the most
perfect and pure sensibility can solve.    Samuel
Butler once suggested that the real test of literary
power was whether a man could name a kitten.
And " by this test," he added, " I am condemned,
for I cannot."    But in his lyrics Blake passes many
and more difficult tests of the same kind.    The
poems on " The Lamb " and " Infant Joy " continually avert disaster as if by a miracle.    The
abysses of silliness and sentimentality which lie in
wait for anyone who wishes to write in this strain,
and in the manner of the following lines :

> *My mother bore me in the southern wild,*
> *And I am black, but O ! my soul is white . . .*

are too obvious to need illustration.    It is more to
the point to notice how skilfully Blake avoids
absurdity, and rescues himself from the trite
metaphors of moral instruction by moving, with
the minutest possible adjustments and the greatest
economy of means, into a more remote and
romantic territory.    The phrase " the southern
wild " admits just as much of romantic and

poetical associations as is necessary to effect the
adjustment. And in the next two lines :

*White as an angel is the English child,*
*But I am black, as if bereav'd of light . . .*

the last line is just sufficiently a conceit to avoid
the obvious and lift the lines into poetry, though
if the reader does not look into it he will see
nothing there except extreme simplicity. And
throughout the *Songs of Innocence* there is the same
extraordinary mixture of naivety and of subtle,
sometimes far-fetched, romantic phrases. It is
the same mixture that we sometimes find in
primitive poetry and ballads, but among the
accomplished poets of later ages hardly any but
Blake and Shakespeare could make it work. And
in the *Songs of Innocence* Blake has so completely
fused these two elements that unless one is alert
one hardly notices in the context how boldly
Blake has compressed his meaning in such images
as " painted birds," " thoughtless nest," and
" under a cruel eye outworn," although the
complicated associations packed into these phrases
always have their effect.

The *Songs of Experience* are even more rich in
elaborately evocative phrases. It is not only in
their mood that they differ from the *Songs of*

*Innocence*, but some of them seem an altogether
different kind of poetry, which comes, as it were,
from a different part of the mind.  In the *Songs
of Innocence*, whatever is below the surface is most
carefully hidden, but many of the *Songs of Experience* seem to refer far more directly to the depths
of the mind.  In " The Sunflower," for example,
there is nothing which does not belong to that
mysterious and remote world of which, in the
*Songs of Innocence*, there is only here and there
a hint.  And a large proportion of the *Songs of
Experience*, though there are still several which
appear simple, as though addressed to children,
are packed with recondite suggestions of mystery.

> *O rose, thou art sick !*
> *The invisible worm*
> *That flies in the night,*
> *In the howling storm,*
>
> *Has found out thy bed*
> *Of crimson joy,*
> *And his dark secret love*
> *Does thy life destroy.*

With the *Songs of Experience* should be read the
earlier poems in the Rossetti MS., a sketch-book
and note-book which Blake used at intervals from
1793 to 1818.  Some of these are only rough drafts
Db

for poems in the *Songs of Experience*, but there are several new poems in which, in Blake's words, there

> . . . *spreads the dismal shade*
> *Of Mystery over his head ;*
> *And the Catterpiller & Fly*
> *Feed on the Mystery.*

Dismal it may be – for the general impression of these poems is of a brooding and calamitous intensity – but perhaps it is in these shadows that Blake is most perfectly an artist. The style is most fully developed in a little book of pictures and verses with the title *For Children : The Gates of Paradise*, which was engraved in 1793, though it was subsequently re-engraved, with some additions and the rather more appropriate title, *For the Sexes : The Gates of Paradise* :

> *On the shadows of the Moon*
> *Climbing thro' Night's highest Noon.*
> *In Time's Ocean falling drown'd.*
> *In Aged Ignorance profound,*
> *Holy & cold, I clip'd the Wings*
> *Of all Sublunary Things,*
> *And in depths of my Dungeons*
> *Closed the Father & the Sons.*
> *But when once I did descry*
> *The Immortal Man that cannot Die,*

*Thro' evening shades I haste away*
*To close the Labours of my Day.*
*The Door of Death I open found*
*And the Worm Weaving in the Ground :*
*Thou'rt my Mother from the Womb,*
*Wife, Sister, Daughter, to the Tomb,*
*Weaving to Dreams the Sexual strife*
*And weeping over the Web of Life.*

It is superb, but it is on the edge of nonsense and
disconnection, and it is hard to imagine that anyone would continue writing in such a manner all
his life.  It seems to be the product of an unstable
equilibrium of the mind, and it is perhaps to this
that it owes its ominous intensity.

# CHAPTER III

Blake's mysticism and philosophy – *The Marriage of Heaven and Hell* – *Visions of the Daughters of Albion* – his revolutionary friends – he rescues an ill-treated boy – his personal appearance – Sir Joshua Reynolds – removal to Lambeth – Thomas Butts – his work as an engraver and treatment of his patrons.

IT is obvious that something of great importance had happened to Blake, at any rate within his own mind, between the time of the *Songs of Innocence* and of the *Songs of Experience*. Mr. Foster Damon, who is anxious to make Blake run on the rails of a mystic way laid down by Miss Evelyn Underhill, thinks that Blake underwent an experience common to all mystics. Mr. Wicksteed, who has interpreted the simpler as Mr. Damon has the more complicated of Blake's works, considers, more practically, that Blake had fallen in love with someone other than his wife. And, indeed, he does find in the *Songs of Experience* and elsewhere a great deal of internal evidence which suggests that Blake longed to take a mistress but probably desisted when he found that his wife was jealous. There is also some slight external evidence for supposing that he proposed to add a concubine to his household. But there is always the possibility that Blake's mind pursued its own internal development without much reference to any events outside his mind, and whatever went on outside his mind always assumed a new form within it. It is a pity that we do not know much about this period of his life except what can be hazardously inferred from his works.

It was certainly during this time that Blake first became thoroughly convinced that the nature of the world ought to be changed. He had had, no doubt, vague desires for a new heaven and a new earth before, but it was now that he began to work them out. *The Book of Thel* was engraved at the same time as the *Songs of Innocence*, and this must certainly be described as a prophetic book, although here Blake's mysticism assumes the benign and gentle character of the songs. The virgin Thel utters no more than " gentle lamentations " that life is vain, and the lily of the valley, the cloud, the worm, and the clod of clay rise up and explain that God cherishes every living thing, and that " we live not for ourselves alone." But there is another section to the poem in which Blake begins his familiar complaints about the intolerable nature of the universe. *Tiriel*, written about the same time, is a far more substantial piece of mythology whose precise import may well be left either to mystics or to psycho-analysts to interpret.

But it is fairly obvious that this history of the tyrant Tiriel and his rebellious children expresses a violent dissatisfaction with something or other. And it is one of the first of those many writings of Blake which, in direct contrast to the lyrics, are loose and straggling, full of diffuse rhetoric and strained images.

Fortunately, Blake shortly afterwards wrote *The Marriage of Heaven and Hell,* his most important prose work, from which it is at least possible to understand some of his preoccupations without recourse to an interpretation, which must always seem arbitrary, of his symbols. At this time Blake had been reading Swedenborg and disagreeing with him, because, while Swedenborg pretended to expose the fallacy of the normal religious use of moral distinctions, he was infected with the same error. And in *The Marriage of Heaven and Hell* Blake seeks to abolish such a distinction. He attacks the schematic dichotomies of religions, such as body and soul, good and evil, and the like, and he observes that God and the Devil are almost interchangeable terms, a fact which Dr. Freud has subsequently noticed. And " all Deities," he says, " reside in the human breast." Thus it is apparently one of the most completely sceptical works ever written, and Blake's criticism is the more devastating because it is throughout

informed with an extraordinary insight into the
psychology of religion.  But, having discovered
the essentially subjective character of religious
and ethical beliefs – "one Law," he says, "for the
Lion and Ox is oppression " – Blake proceeds,
both here and elsewhere, to deny the existence
of all evil.  There was, it would seem, a confusion in his mind between good and evil as
applied to the moral nature of thoughts and
actions, and the same terms as used to describe
those events which cause pleasure or pain to
human beings.  Having denied, for instance, that
lust is in itself evil – " the lust of the goat is the
bounty of God " – he sees no reason why desires
not in themselves evil should lead to actions which
sometimes have painful, hence evil, consequences,
or, indeed, why there should be any evil consequences in the world at all.  Thus laws, which
check desires not in themselves evil, are intolerable, and Blake comes to believe that without
laws, churches, or restrictions the world would be
happy.  It seems to be because he had to fight
against this and many other dilemmas that, after
remarking that " all Deities reside in the human
breast," he peopled his universe with rather more
supernatural beings than most religions employ.
But in any case he could never have sustained
total scepticism for long – at a later date he

described himself as " mad as a refuge from unbelief." In poems written about the same time as *The Marriage of Heaven and Hell*, he ventured to call the Supreme Being " old Nobodaddy aloft," using a portmanteau word composed of "nobody" and " daddy." But when, much later, he read a poem by Wordsworth in which the poet says that he passed the hosts of Jehovah unalarmed, Blake was so much distressed that he retired to bed with a complaint of the bowels from which, as he said, he very nearly died. But he never ceased to dislike priests. Having read, late in his life, in Sir Joshua Reynolds's *Discourses*, that some-one " had been originally a Dissenting minister," he was moved to write " Villainy ! " in the margin of the book.

If Mr. Wicksteed is right, it was not long before Blake encountered in his own home a singularly poignant refutation of his theory of evil. If his own desires were not evil – " the lust of the goat is the bounty of God " – why should he not indulge them without evil consequences ? But the evil consequences were there :

*A flower was offer'd to me,*
  *Such a flower as May never bore ;*
*But I said " I've a pretty Rose-tree,"*
  *And I passed the sweet flower o'er.*

*Then I went to my Pretty Rose-tree,*
*To tend her by day and by night ;*
*But my Rose turn'd away with jealousy,*
*And her thorns were my only delight.*

Nothing remained for Blake to do but to endow
the tragedy with a cosmic setting, which he pro-
ceeded to do in *Visions of the Daughters of Albion.*
This seems to be a long complaint of the horrors
of jealousy, but the sufferers are more than mortal,
and here it is a male being who suffers from
jealousy while his consort, who is described as the
spirit of America (then, because of the War of
Independence, the land of the free), is willing to
allow him every freedom and even to provide him
with " girls of mild silver or of furious gold."
And, she continues :

*I'll lie beside thee on the bank & view their wanton*
*play.* . . .

Not only America, but France – for this was
the time of the French Revolution – seemed a
possible paradise of freedom to Blake, and in 1791
he wrote a long poem on the French Revolution
in seven books.  It was the only work of his which
ever found a publisher – it was accepted by Johnson, a bookseller of revolutionary inclinations –

and, even so, only the first book ever found its way into print, and then it probably got no farther than proof-sheets. Only this first book remains, and Swinburne described it, with some reason, as " consisting mainly of mere wind and splutter." It certainly illustrates in an extreme form the faults of all the prophctic books. It is as diffuse and repetitive as the lyrics are compact, and the far-fetched images which occur at times in the lyrics are here both infinitely more frequent and usually empty of content. As Blake had done before, but now far more thoroughly, he gives to every historical event which he describes an apocalyptic significance.

At Johnson's shop – for at this time the intelligentsia were accustomed to use booksellers' shops as clubs – Blake made the acquaintance of Johnson's revolutionary friends, including Mary Wollestonecraft, Godwin, and Paine. Blake became a great admirer of Paine, and in a copy of Bishop Watson's apology for the Bible which he was reading at this time he frequently wrote down, among many other annotations, that Paine was much more like Christ than was the Bishop. " Christ died an unbeliever," he wrote, for he was still firmly sceptical, " and if the Bishops had their way so would Paine." But Blake had an opportunity of saving Paine's life. Paine was

describing to the company an inflammatory
speech which he had made the evening before,
and at a time when he was already threatened
with a Government prosecution for his book on
the Rights of Man. Blake told him that if he
went home he would be " a dead man." And
in fact the police were already in Paine's house,
and he only just escaped to France, an order for
his arrest arriving at Dover twenty minutes after
his boat had sailed. It is clear that Blake could
on occasion be very astute.

He was sufficiently impressed by these revolutionaries to wear a red cap in the streets, but it is
said that he did not take to Godwin, finding in
him that spirit of cold reasoning which was always
his bugbear. Godwin once boasted to Coleridge
that he had carried on an argument with the
scholar Mackintosh for three hours without coming
to any particular conclusion. " If there had been
a man of genius in the room," answered Coleridge,
" he would have settled the question in five minutes." And no doubt Blake was just such a man of
genius, and effectively interrupted Godwin's arguments. Nevertheless, the spectacle of Blake among
the philosophers, the admirers of reason, is an odd
one. But Dr. Priestley, the discoverer of oxygen,
who was one of their number, was at least so much
connected with the Swedenborgians, and hence

with mysticism, that he attacked them.   And
Mary Wollestonecraft, to whose *Original Stories
from Real Life* Blake contributed six illustrations,
seems to have aroused Blake's sympathy both for
herself and for her love-affairs.   It was during this
time, when she was meeting the other revolutionaries at dinner in Johnson's room above his
shop, that she proposed herself as a " spiritual
concubine " to the painter Fuseli, but was rejected
by Fuseli's wife.   It has been suggested that
Blake's poem " Mary " was written about Mary
Wollestonecraft, and, if this is so, it is clear that
Blake both admired and sympathised with her,
and perhaps that he thought her character and
fate like his own.   For in the poem she is made
to say :

> *O, why was I born with a different Face ?*
> *Why was I not born like this Envious Race ?*
> *Why did Heaven adorn me with bountiful hand,*
> *And then set me down in an envious Land ?*

And at the end of the poem, Blake addresses her
thus :

> *And thine is a Face of sweet Love in despair,*
> *And thine is a Face of mild sorrow & care,*
> *And thine is a Face of wild terror & fear*
> *That shall never be quiet till laid on its bier.*

Blake was no abstract humanitarian, and was never content to work out the logical arguments for freedom. His biographer, Tatham, gives an anecdote which admirably illustrates, not only his enthusiasm, but his courage. It was precisely such a test of his principles as most of us are careful to avoid, and the embarrassment, if not the risk, would be too much for us. It is not the kind of thing which any literary man can be expected to do. But Blake suffered from no inhibitions and showed no hesitation. He was standing at one of the windows of his house in Lambeth which looked into the premises of a theatre kept by a certain Astley, and called by his name. There he saw a boy hobbling along with a log tied to his foot, " such an one as is put on a horse or ass to prevent them straying." He called his wife and asked her what it meant, and she explained that it must be a punishment " for some in-advertence." At once " Blake's blood boiled and his indignation surpassed his forbearance." He rushed out and " demanded in no very quiescent terms that the boy should be loosed, and that no Englishman should be subjected to these miseries, which he thought inexcusable, even towards a slave." He was, indeed, so impressive that he succeeded in obtaining the boy's release and went quietly home. But by this time Astley himself had come to hear of Blake's interference, and came to his house demanding " in an equally peremptory manner, by what authority he dared come athwart his method of jurisdiction. To which Blake replied with such warmth that blows were very nearly the consequence." There was, in fact, a most painful scene, just such a scene as most of us all too vividly anticipate when we meditate rushing in to put our principles into practice. But here again Blake was exceptional, and rose superbly to the situation. He succeeded in calming and convincing Astley, who " saw that his punishment was too degrading, and admired Blake for his humane sensibility." And Tatham is able to conclude the anecdote with this admirable moral : that " if all quarrels were thus settled, the time would shortly come when the lion would lie down with the lamb, and the little child should lead them." Unhappily, Blake had few opportunities of taking such practical steps to bring on either his own or Tatham's millennium.

Blake himself was inclined to attribute his revolutionary opinions to his personal appearance ; the shape of his forehead, he thought, made him a republican. " I can't help being one," he would explain to his Tory friends, " any more than you can help being a Tory : your forehead is larger above : mine, on the contrary, over the eyes." And certainly such a being as Tatham describes must have been impetuous, uninhibited, and bold. " Elasticity and promptitude of action were the characteristics of his contour." His eyes were fiery ; they were " large, dark and impressive," and with them " he seemed to look into another world." An old man who had only seen him once remembered all his life how his eyes had flashed with indignation. His hair was yellow brown ; it " stood up like a curling flame, and looked at a distance like radiations." It is true that he was short of stature, but so well made and proportioned that " West, the great history painter, admired much the form of his limbs." His movements were always quick and energetic ; he was very strong, and he could never sit still without something to do in his hands. He had a snub nose, a distinction to which he himself often alluded and which he appears to have thought of some importance. " I have always thought," he says, " that Jesus Christ was a Snubby, or I should not have worship'd him, if I had thought he had been one of those long spindle-nosed rascals." He dressed in a sedate and sober fashion, in black, " something like an old-fashioned tradesman's dress," but looking like " a gentleman, in a way of his own."

All the while, amidst all this ferment of new

thought, Blake worked conscientiously and laboriously as an engraver, and made his living entirely by this trade. In Poland Street he lived next door to Reynolds, and called on him to show his designs. The great man recommended Blake to correct his drawing and modify his extravagances, at which he was mortally offended. But it is also said that when they met, each, to his own surprise, found the other agreeable. "Well, Mr. Blake," Reynolds said, "I hear you despise our art of oil-painting." "No, Sir Joshua," Blake answered, "I don't despise it ; but I like fresco better." Nevertheless, Blake always detested Reynolds's opinions and his paintings ; he used the paint-brush far too energetically, and was too confirmed a generaliser, for Blake to approve either his precepts or his practice. On his copy of Reynolds's *Discourses* Blake wrote :

"This man was hired to depress Art : this is the opinion of William Blake. My proofs of this opinion are given in the following notes. . . . Having spent the vigour of my youth and genius under the oppression of Sir Joshua, and his gang of cunning, hired knaves – without employment, and, as much as could possibly be, without bread – the reader must expect to read, in all my remarks on

these books, nothing but indignation and resent-
ment.  While Sir Joshua was rolling in riches,
Barry was poor and unemployed, except by his
own energy ;  Mortimer was called a madman,
and only portrait painting was applauded and
rewarded by the rich and great.  Reynolds and
Gainsborough blotted and blurred one against
the other, and divided all the English world
between them.  Fuseli, indignant, almost hid
himself.  I AM HID."

Barry was a pupil of Reynolds, an historical painter, and in early life Blake imitated Mortimer,
who was considered the finest historical painter
of his own time, with a great reputation, as
Gilchrist puts it, " for fancy and correct drawing
of the human figure."  Blake chose unfortunate
examples of the sublime and the beautiful, but
there is some justice in his complaints of the state
of English painting and English patronage.

In 1792 he moved to Lambeth, then a suburb,
where he had a pleasant house with a garden and
a vine which, naturally enough, he refused on
principle to prune.  Here he passed the most
prosperous years of his life.  Indeed, he was now
so rich that when thieves broke into his house they
carried away plate to the value of £60 and clothes
to the value of £40 more, and Blake lent another

E B

£40 to a free-thinking philosopher, whose wife at once bought a new dress, which she flaunted in front of the Blakes. Blake added to his income by giving drawing lessons, and had pupils of high rank whom he so much delighted with his conversation that they often persuaded him to stay on for the rest of the day after the lesson was over. But when he was offered the position of drawing-master to the Royal Family, he saw that it was time to stop. With all his taste for eccentric company, this was too much. And perhaps it was as well, for when George the Third was shown some of Blake's drawings, that difficult critic only exclaimed, " Take them away. . . .Take them away."

Blake's prosperity was much increased by discovering the perfect patron. Thomas Butts seems to have been a charming character, infinitely mild and kind, who kept Blake as a pet without ever offending him. He liked to make little jokes about Blake, and thoroughly enjoyed his eccentricity. When addressed as " Dear Friend of My Angels," he wrote in answer that he could never tell whether Blake's angels were devils, or his devils angels. And Butts was delighted to find Blake and his wife sitting in an Arcadian arbour under the vine-tree reading *Paradise Lost*, " in character." When he showed some natural

hesitation, " Come in," said Blake ; " it is only
Adam and Eve." It is a simple and most probable story, for there were at this time the begin-
nings of a " nudist " movement in England, but it
has caused extreme anguish to many of Blake's
critics. Mr. Graham Robertson seeks to throw
doubt on the story by arguing that when Blake
used to tell people that he was Socrates or Isaiah,
" no change of costume was necessary to assist
his imagination." No, but perhaps some change
of costume was necessary to assist the imagination
of Mr. Butts. Swinburne denies the whole story
in a torrent of outraged rhetoric. And Mr.
Ellis comforts himself with the thought that,
since Blake was nothing if not accurate, he and
his wife may have been wearing the " coats of
skin made by the Lord " for Adam and Eve. In
any case, it is Butts, not the poet, who is to
blame :

" He remains the only person really disgraced
by it. Gilchrist [who repeated the story] is but
lightly smirched in comparison. After all, Blake
and his wife *were married*. And there is still the
question of the coats of skin made by the Lord."

But, even so, Mr. Ellis has not come to the end of
his resources. Blake and his wife, he suggests,

probably undressed in the summer-house and were not such monsters as to go all the way down the garden path from their house without their clothes. But, whatever may be the precise degree of his own or of Blake's indelicacy, Butts evidently enjoyed the episode, and continued to buy a picture a week, only pausing when he had no more room in his house.

Blake's largest work at this time was to illustrate Young's *Night Thoughts*. It was not, perhaps, the kind of poem of which he approved, though he must have approved of the manner in which Young, as he explained in his *Conjectures on Original Composition*, composed by pure inspiration. Indeed, the *Night Thoughts*, presumably because of its author's trust in inspiration, is one of the few English works included by the French *Surréalistes* in their list of past works which accord with their principles. For this poem Blake made 537 designs, but only the first part of the edition was published, with 43 engravings. It was a comparative failure.

Nevertheless, Blake was beginning to acquire a reputation both as an engraver and as an artist. Farington noted in his diary that " West, Cosway and Humphrey spoke warmly of the designs of Blake the Engraver, as works of extraordinary genius and imagination." Yet Blake was not an easy employee. Much of the work by which he gained his living was of a menial, journeyman kind, but 'e could never bring himself to treat it as such. A sober, undistinguished clergyman, John Trusler, author of a treatise on *The Way to be Rich and Respectable*, was introduced to Blake, and wished to employ him in illustrating his books with suitable and intelligible plates. Naturally the designs which he sent in were of no use, but he would not alter them. " I am really sorry," he wrote to the clergyman, " that you are fallen out with the spiritual world," and he continued with a magnificent profession of his faith in imagination :

" I feel that a man may be happy in this world, and I know that this world is a world of imagination and vision. I see everything I paint in this world but everybody does not see alike. To the eyes of a miser a guinea is far more beautiful than the sun, and a bag worn with the use of money has more beautiful proportions than a vine filled with grapes. The tree which moves some to tears of joy is in the eyes of others only a green thing which stands in the way. Some see Nature all ridicule and deformity, and by these I shall not regulate my proportions ; and some scarce see Nature at all. But to the eyes of the man of imagination,

Nature is Imagination itself.  As a man is, so he
sees.  As the eye is formed, such are its powers.
You certainly mistake, when you say that the
visions of fancy are not to be found in this world.
To me this world is all one continued vision of
fancy or imagination, and I feel flattered when
I am told so.  What is it sets Homer, Virgil, and
Milton in so high a rank of art ?  Why is the Bible
more entertaining and instructive than any other
book ?  Is it not because they are addressed to the
imagination, which is spiritual sensation, and but
mediately to the understanding or reason ?  Such
is true painting, and such was valued alone by
the Greeks and the best modern artists."

But, however magnificent, it was entirely
inappropriate, and one can hardly be surprised
that Trusler wrote on the letter, " Blake, dim'd
with superstition."

For Blake had no notion how to compromise
with the Philistines and keep his imagination to
himself ; he could not market his competence and
keep back his genius.  Even when his task was to
decorate the announcement of a sale of " the
greatest variety of carpets from the lowest Scotch
and Kidderminster, Wilton and Brussels to the
finest Axminster, Turkey and Persia," he had to

let himself go and invent symbolical sublimities illustrating the more visionary aspects of the carpet trade. " I live," he said at this time, " by miracle," and it is indeed a miracle that he should have earned his living at all. And yet he obviously took a pleasure in modest craftsmanship, when he was not carried away by his ideas, and this probably preserved him on his way. " I have no objection," he wrote in the same letter to Trusler, " to engraving after another artist. Engraving is the profession I was apprenticed to, and should never have attempted to live by anything else if orders had not come in for my designs and paintings." It was, one may infer, when he had to make his own designs that he was least able to control his imagination, but even when he engraved from other artists he could not always forbear to add some touch of visionary splendour.

And so he continued, selling enough pictures and engravings to live in moderate comfort and just, but only just, controlling his imagination so that it did not seriously interfere with the practice of his trade. He was probably living almost entirely in a world invented by himself, but he could manage his own affairs. When he began to write, he moved at once into this other world of his imagination and poured out the prophetic books, which he continued to write almost until the last days of his life, working mostly at night, under the evident influence of inspiration, and taking down what the voices of angels dictated to him as fast as he could write.

# CHAPTER IV

The prophetic books – Blake's archæological and other theories
– his insanity – criticism of his painting and engraving.

IT is an adventure to look into the prophetic
books. Godlike beings assault our ears with their
superhuman lamentations, or persuade us to
share their heaven of divine exaltation. We are
startled by the extraordinary variety and intricacy
of their sexual behaviour.

*The howlings, gnashings, groanings, shriekings, shud-*
*derings, sobbings, burstings*
*Mingle together to create a world. . . .*

And it is a world which seems to be an infinite
height above the concerns of common humanity
or the familiar features of this earth. All natural
phenomena are on a terrific scale, all animals are
fabulous monsters, all vegetation " fibres of life,"
or even capable, like " Albion's tree," of " Athe-
istical, Epicurean Philosophy." But suddenly,
with a fascinating rapidity, we descend to earth,
and the local geography of England, even the
streets of London, form a part of this dread
universe of discord.

73

*The Corner of Broad Street weeps; Poland Street languishes;*
*To Great Queen Street & Lincoln's Inn all is distress & woe.*

And with names like Los, Orc, Palamobron, Golgonooza, at once profoundly mysterious and slightly absurd, there mingle incongruously Skofeld, the name of a private soldier with whom Blake had a quarrel, Slade, Kox, Peachey, and other obscure persons.

Several attempts have been made to extract order from this chaos and to interpret Blake's innumerable and baffling symbols. Of these interpretations, the most elaborate and systematic is that of Mr. Foster Damon, who believes that Blake never failed to wrest "some great Truth from the Eternity which he entered." But everyone knows those great Truths with a capital T, and how puzzling and obscure they are – perhaps, in the last resort, as puzzling as the prophetic books. This, for example, is a specimen of Mr. Damon's interpretation :

"There is a negative work in the process of salvation which is hardly less important. To acquire Truth, one must cast out Error. Error consists of all Illusions, Prohibitions, and

Negations, which of their very nature have no
real existence.  A Contrary, as Blake warns us, is
not a Negation, but a positive thing.  Contraries
must be reconciled ; for if one Contrary is
rejected, the domination of its fellow ensues,
and Truth is divided.  Negations, however, are
illusions.  All such Errors are Devils.  The
greatest Error is Satan, the Accuser.  He springs
from Selfhood – or rather, ' selfishness,' for Blake
never denied the Individual . . . " etc., etc.

A faint flavour of Christian Science – error is
the significant word – may possibly be detected
in this passage, but even this hardly clears up
its meaning.  This may have been what Blake
wanted to say, but, if so, Mr. Damon's *précis* only
plunges us into deeper obscurity.  Philosophical
notions, when used in this way, are to some
minds even more difficult to understand than
the adventures of Palamobron.  Mr. Wicksteed,
whose interpretations are in general much more
comprehensible, especially when he relates Blake's
works to the events of his life, can still confuse us
when he comes to a " significant though cryptic
line in *Jerusalem*," which is :

" *All things Begin & End in Albion's Ancient Druid
    Rocky Shore.*"

" This being expanded," he tells us, " amounts
to saying that howsoever we may explore the
realms of vision we must come back in the end
to that hard and narrow age-long way that skirts
the margin between Time and Eternity, where
Druid sacrifice of humanity is common, but
which is for every man his native earth." Here,
it seems to me, Mr. Wicksteed has not made
things any easier, and the more so since this line,
with the aid of M. Denis Saurat's discoveries
about Blake's beliefs and those common at his
time, is not one of the most difficult to understand. M. Saurat has pointed out that it was a
common belief in the eighteenth century, a
belief which has analogies with the opinions of
the British Israelites and was maintained by the
same sort of people who nowadays trust the
prophetic powers of the great pyramid, that both
Greek philosophy and the religion of the Jews
sprang originally from the Druids in England, or,
as was held in France, from the Gauls or Celts of
France. Thus Blake is quite simply giving expression to a common archæological theory, one
to which even Milton, as a patriot, inclined, for
in the *Areopagetica* he says that " writers of good
antiquity and able judgement have been persuaded that even the school of Pythagoras and the
Persian wisdom took beginning from the old

BLAKE

philosophy of this island." Blake also believed,
as this line implies, that, just as everything began
on Albion's Druid shore, so there will be a
millennium when everything will end there. And
it seems probable that a good many of his more
obscure passages are so difficult to understand
because they refer to some matter about which
we now know nothing – either, as with Skofeld,
some event in his life, or some half-witted, half-
mystical theory like that which maintains the
Druid origin of all culture. And M. Saurat has
discovered adumbrations of many such theories
in the prophetic books, theories which were
maintained by many others in the eighteenth
century. " The more we study Blake," M.
Saurat says, " the more persuaded we become
that there was not one absurdity in Europe at
the end of the eighteenth century that Blake did
not know."

M. Saurat has proved as convincingly as may
be that Blake was actually a British Israelite.
The English are the ten lost tribes – that is, the
Jews originally sprang from England, but left
there after a Fall, something like the original
Fall of the Bible. Blake even goes so far as to
divide the counties of England among the tribes
of Israel. In the millennium there will be a
New Jerusalem, when the Jews will all return

to England.  Addressing himself to the Jews,
Blake writes :

"Jerusalem the Emanation of the Giant
Albion !  Can it be ?  Is it a Truth that the
Learned have explored ?  Was Britain the Primitive Seat of the Patriarchal Religion ? . . . It
is True and cannot be controverted.

Even that famous and beautiful lyric from the
prophetic book *Milton* – " And did those feet in
ancient time . . . " – which makes so irresistible
an appeal as a peculiarly happy combination of
religious and nationalist sentiment, merely ex-
pounds the same archæological theory, and when
the pious sing with genuine fervour :

> *I will not cease from Mental Fight,*
> *Nor shall my Sword sleep in my hand*
> *Till we have built Jerusalem*
> *In England's green and pleasant Land . . .*

they little know to what gross and mortal heresy
they are subscribing.  If we read the whole poem
with this knowledge of Blake's beliefs, it is difficult
to understand how any other interpretation could
be put upon it.  It is quite true that Blake was
mysteriously able to colour a preposterous theory
with genuine and, in this instance, sublime

emotions, but this hardly alters the actual and intentional meaning of the poem. The British Israelite Movement probably meant something to Blake which it does not now mean to most of its adherents. It was a path by which deep and obscure emotions could somehow express themselves, but it is of no use to ignore the actual nature of this path.

The difficulty of understanding the prophetic books is that we seldom know when Blake's statements are to be taken literally, as matters of fact " which the learned have explored " about the past or future history of the world, or when he is using symbols, metaphors, or allegories. And he was apt to confuse in a most difficult and subtle manner his literal statements with allegories and his allegories with literal statements. Thus he wove his theories about the Jews and the Druids into his own mythology inextricably and in a most confusing fashion. And even his symbols and allegories may refer obliquely, by way of his views on the nature of the universe, to his own emotions, or they may refer more directly to them, as in the earlier books, where he is preoccupied with the problems aroused by jealousy and infidelity. In general, as time went on, he tended to refer more and more obliquely to his own desires and emotions, disguising them

more and more effectually as statements about
the nature of the univ**e**rse. We can just understand the personal problems with which he is
struggling in *The Visions of the Daughters of
Albion*, but it would take all the skill of the
most ingenious psycho-analyst to detect them in
*Jerusalem.*

This method of struggling with mental conflicts
by pushing them outside the mind into eternity,
heaven, or the universe, is a very familiar one.
It is practised, of course, by the larger part of the
human race. But a few people who practise it
either in too emphatic or too consistent a fashion
are considered mad, and may or may not be
locked up in an asylum. Yet it is a curious fact
that there is no essential difference in the character
of the beliefs held by those who are considered
mad and by those who are not. Those who believe
that the English are the lost tribes may very well
not be considered mad, but the asylums are full
of people holding rather similar beliefs. Thus,
since the distinction between the mad and the
sane appears to be perfectly arbitrary, it would
seem foolish to enquire whether or no Blake was
mad, a question which all his critics feel bound to
discuss. But in fact there is often a difference
between the behaviour of those who are called
mad and of those who are called sane, though

there is often no great difference in the nature of their beliefs.

It is true that the distinction appears to be largely social. Nietzsche observed that madness is an exception among individuals but the rule in societies, and it is when an individual has his own delusions, and not those of the society to which he belongs, even though his own delusions may not differ from those which are held by other societies, that he is considered mad. But this distinction is not quite so arbitrary as it looks. The mind of a person who has his own delusions rather than those of any society, or section of society, to which he belongs, is likely to be less in contact with anything outside it than the mind of someone who merely accepts the delusions of his fellow-men. For society is a part of the outside world, and to take notice of its opinions, to be infected by its delusions, is at least to be aware of something other than one's own fantasies. There must, of course, be many border-line cases. There are, for instance, those who take the delusions of a society rather more literally than they are meant to be taken. There is the class of those whose opinions happen to be verifiable but violently conflict with the opinions of a society which does not want to verify them. And, finally, there is the very interesting class of those who

FB

succeed in infecting society with their beliefs, even though they may be their own invention and obviously unverifiable. Thus Mr. James Strachey speaks of " the schizophrenic prophet Ezekiel " – a diagnosis made on the basis of Ezekiel's delusions – but it is a judgment which would be violently resented by those who have been persuaded to subscribe to Ezekiel's beliefs. It is to this last class that Blake must belong. It can hardly be denied that the majority of his opinions were unverifiable, and that many of them, though fewer than was thought before M. Denis Saurat's discoveries, were his own invention. Yet he succeeded in infecting a few people with them in his lifetime, and a large number after his death.

Thus nearly all Blake's critics are vigorously opposed to the theory, maintained by several who knew Blake and at intervals by Blake himself, that he was mad. Mr. Wicksteed speaks of his " mighty sanity." " It would be well," says Miss Mona Wilson, " for those who are so eager to charge genius with madness, to remember that they lay themselves open to the suspicion of being mentally defective." " It would be cruel," Mr. Foster Damon says, " to print even the names of those hearty critics who have frankly proclaimed Blake mad because they could not understand him." Mr. Lytton Strachey, in the course of an extraordinarily acute and sensitive essay on Blake's poetry, suggests that no madman would be capable of " that sort of consistency which lies in the repeated enunciation of the same body of beliefs throughout a large mass of compositions and over a long period of time." Unfortunately, " that sort of consistency " might almost be a definition of certain kinds of madness. But in the face of so formidable a body of opinion one hesitates to lay oneself open " to the suspicion of being mentally defective," at any rate on a purely social definition of madness.

There are, however, other ways of judging madness. As we have seen, a man with private delusions may differ from a man with social and shared delusions because he is more impervious to anything outside his mind, more enclosed in the world of his own fantasies and desires. And it happens to be characteristic of a certain kind of lunacy (to which the name " schizophrenia," meaning " split mind," is given) to invent a complicated delusional universe, which is often very much like that which Blake invents in his prophetic books. The name " schizophrenia " does not imply a split personality, but that the mind is split away from reality, its attention is distracted from the outside world, and it works as it were, by itself. Within its confines, and using premises which are not checked by comparison with any facts, the mind may work very intelligently, in much the same way as the scholastic philosophers worked, deducing a vast system from premises whose truth they did not attempt to verify or to doubt. Dr. Lionel Penrose, writing in *The British Journal of Medical Psychology*, Part I., 1931, gives a fascinating account of the delusional universe of a schizophrenic of eighty years of age who had spent fifty years in the construction of it. Dr. Penrose was able to question the old gentleman, and so, being in a much better position than Blake's critics, he was able to make this universe appear rather more consistent and comprehensible than that of Blake's prophetic books. The analogies with Blake's universe are many and striking. There is an elaborate symbolical geography resembling that which Blake constructs in *Jerusalem*, with places whose position is connected with moral attributes. There is a millennium in which the world is to be rebuilt on a definite plan. And this universe is inhabited by many semi-mythological personages with fantastic names (the patient had a passion for neologisms of all kinds) resembling those of Blake's creation. It is true that the patient's interests were more mathematical than Blake's – he invented new systems of measurement and a new calendar – but Blake, being a poet and painter, was inclined to attribute to these arts the cosmic importance which this patient attributed to his systems of measurement. And with all his fantastic delusions the patient, although a quite uneducated man, was exceptionally intelligent. His calendar and measurements required the most elaborate calculations which, being blind, he had to do in his head.

Nor are the prophetic books the sole evidence of Blake's state of mind. In fact, there is so much that one hardly knows what to choose. Perhaps the descriptive catalogue of the exhibition of his pictures, which he held in 1809, will do. For here his delusions have broken loose from the comparatively safe compartment which his imaginative works provided for them. There are, of course, mysterious allusions to Druids, Ancient Britains, and other curiosities of archæology. And there are many such assertions as that " no man can believe that either Homer's Mythology, or Ovid's, were the production of Greece or Latium," perhaps because they are so obviously the production of British Druids. But these are social delusions, differing only in degree but not in kind from the more guarded raptures of other patriots on the subject of English painting or the English countryside. Blake, after all, only says that he believes, " with Milton, the ancient British

History." But there are many indications of more private delusions, and there are definite signs that a persecution mania had overtaken him. The bugbear chiaroscuro comes in again, but now it is "in the hands of Venetian and Flemish Demons," who are described as having "an enmity to the Painter himself." "The Spirit of Titian was particularly active in raising doubts." "Rubens is a most outrageous demon." As to one picture, "fortunately, or rather, providentially, he [Blake] left it unblotted and unblurred, although molested continually by blotting and blurring demons." And there are many more or less hysterical complaints against human persecutors. By the time of this exhibition he had been disappointed in his hopes of public recognition, which helps to explain the bitterness which enters into his delusions. I see no reason to suppose that Blake was using metaphors in a normal way when he spoke of devils, or writing playfully. The exhibition was intended to make a bid for public reputation, and if he had been able to he would surely have taken care to keep his fantasies from the public eye, and he would have been scrupulous to avoid suggesting to his audience what in fact the catalogue instantly suggested to the art critic of the *Examiner* – that the pictures were the work of a lunatic. There is, perhaps, a faint veil of conscious

extravagance and humour, as if Blake was aware
that he must not expose himself too much, over
the megalomania which is still obvious enough in
a passage from a project for a public address,
composed at the same time as the catalogue of the
exhibition. He is speaking of the painters whom
he dislikes :

" If all the Princes in Europe, like Louis XIV
& Charles the first, were to Patronize such Block-
heads, I, William Blake, a Mental Prince, should
decollate & Hang their Souls as Guilty of Mental
High Treason."

But there seems no trace of any conscious humour
in most of the catalogue.

Some years after this exhibition Crabb Robinson
had many conversations with Blake, and recorded
them in his diary. Robinson was of the opinion
that Blake was mad, and if his records are accurate
it is hard to doubt it. His description, which
Robinson quoted, of what happened when he
wrote, is not compatible with any kind of sanity.
" I write . . ." he said, " when commanded by the
spirits, and the moment I have written I see the
words fly about in all directions. It is then published, and the spirits can read. My MS. is of no
further use, I have been tempted to burn my MS.
but my wife won't let me." But even at this time,

when it would seem that his delusions had increased in number and strength, he was still affected by the reactions of those to whom he was speaking. Thus, when he said to Robinson, " I was Socrates," he paused and then, " as if correcting himself," added, " A sort of brother. I must have had conversations with him. So I had with Jesus, I have an obscure recollection of having been with both of them." The suggestion is usually made that when Blake was with people likely to disbelieve and exasperate him – Crabb Robinson is given as an example of such a person – he would " say things," as Gilchrist put it, " in order to make people startle and stare." But this conversation with Robinson does not support this view. If Blake had been anxious to tease Robinson he would presumably have started with the mildest assertion and have been drawn on to the most presumptuous. Instead, he seems to have been anxious to apologise for, and to withdraw from, his first wild statement. I do not mean that Blake never talked in order to shock, but these remarks at least cannot be explained in this way. Nor does his description of how the words which he had written flew about the room sound in the least like the kind of thing one would say in order to startle. Anyone who wished to shock Crabb Robinson could think of much better things to say,

and, whatever Blake was, he was never unin-
ventive.

It is possible that so many of Blake's critics and
biographers have so eagerly denied that he was
mad because one usually imagines a lunatic to
be either a kind of Shakespearean fool, gibbering
inconsequent sublimities, or a creature mopping
and mowing with straws in its hair.  But dementia
is only a final stage of schizophrenia to which the
schizophrenic need not necessarily arrive.  There
is, in fact, an unbroken progression from apparent
sanity or normality to lunacy within the meaning
of the act, and there is no sharp dividing-line
between any of the stages.  Miss Mona Wilson is
probably right when she suggests that Blake
" merely cultivated or possessed normal powers
to an extraordinary degree."  Even normal people
only check their beliefs and control their fantasies
by comparison with facts to a very limited extent.
But that Blake controlled his fantasies much less
than the normal person, and in fact not much
more than a good many people now in asylums,
seems to me obvious.  On any other hypothesis his
life and the greater part of his writings seem to me
inexplicable.

It is probable that as time went on Blake
lived increasingly under the domination of his
fantasies, and was less and less able to check them

by comparison with reality. They seem to have escaped his control to some extent during the period between the *Songs of Innocence* and the *Songs of Experience*, and after this time, when they could no longer be at all consistently controlled by the rather mysterious process of converting them to works of art, they got altogether out of hand. But it is interesting to observe that painting, an art which automatically imposes a far more rigid control of fantasy than does literature, still served Blake as a sublimation, and continued to do so till the end of his life. His pictures are often intimately connected with his delusional universe, and they are often almost as much a product of his delusions as the prophetic books. Mr. Wicksteed has shown that Blake's illustrations to the Book of Job should more properly be called illustrations of Blake's own cosmogony. But owing to the peculiar character of this art he was able to control his fantasy and make his pictures intelligible, at least superficially and to the same extent as his lyrics. When Skofeld comes into a picture he is not just a symbol which would be unintelligible if we did not happen to know who Skofeld was, and even then is not altogether explicable. He is a human figure expressing emotions which everyone can understand, and he is also part of an interesting pattern of shapes and colours.

Unfortunately, Blake lived at the worst of all possible times and was trained in the most unsuitable of all schools for an imaginative painter. The period during which he lived marks the beginning of impressionism, chiefly with Constable but also with earlier anticipations of the movement in the eighteenth century. But with the exact observation of light, of landscape, and of the vegetable universe, Blake was not concerned. In fact he was violently opposed to such modes of painting, and if they had ever presented themselves to his attention he would, if he was to be at all consistent, have rejected them as vigorously as he rejected Venetian and Dutch anticipations of the impressionist technique. It is true that in his old age Blake saw a drawing by Constable and said to the painter, " Why, this is not drawing but Inspiration." But Constable replied, " I meant it for drawing," and so presumably nothing came of the contact. And one can hardly believe that Blake could have thought well of Constable's painting as a whole. But during Blake's life another style came into being which was the exact opposite of impressionism. It is a most curious fact that the gradual progress of the painters of the eighteenth century towards impressionism, as they allowed their pictorial organisations to become more and more random and consequently to admit a closer observation of effects of light without disturbing the design, was violently interrupted by the invention of a rigidly schematic and abstract style. It was a style which allowed none but the most severely generalised facts about the primary properties of matter to be noted. David was its chief and most thoroughgoing exponent, but even in England there were many artists, like Flaxman, who were devoured by a passion for antique sculpture and sought to make everything in their works as abstract and as generalised as antique sculpture seemed to them to be. Blake, with his passion for pure outline, for " the hard and wiry lines of rectitude," and with his vigorous hostility to the chaotic vegetable universe, was inevitably attracted to this style. It was the only current style which seemed to him sufficiently remote from imitation of natural appearances, sufficiently abstract, sufficiently manageable, to make a suitable framework for the parts of his delusional universe. Unfortunately, the style was derived almost entirely from antique sculpture, and it was only in the works of the Greeks and Romans that painters like David could find those aseptic, generalised, almost mathematically describable forms which they required for their own paintings. And, however suitable this was for French revolutionaries who believed in the rule of Reason, one

can imagine no more hopeless style for a visionary
like Blake.  How could Urizen rise up from his
couch to weep

> *. . . in the dark deep, anxious in his scaly form*
> *To reassume the human . . .*

in the disguise of a sleek Antinous or of a Roman
senator ?  It was a difficulty which Blake took a
long time to discover, and at first we find him in
a great state of excitement about " the lost art of
the Greeks," but in the end he did so, and complained that the gods of Greece and Rome were
" mathematical diagrams," which is precisely
what, in the hands of David and Flaxman, they
are.

Whenever he attempted the sort of design which
can be produced from rigidly outlined, almost
geometrical forms, Blake was peculiarly inept.  He
was a master of free, calligraphic line, and when
this freedom was prevented, either by the processes
of engraving (and especially the stiff and laborious
methods of engraving which were taught by
Basire) or by his own taste for sharply outlined
Michelangelesque figures, he was almost certain
to fail.  It is true that his training in the laborious
craft of engraving, and perhaps even his schizophrenic passion for outline, may have kept him

from indulging in too vague a symbolism, from filling his pictures with chaotic and unintelligible symbols chosen for their reference to his delusional universe rather than for their suitability as parts of a design, and, in fact, from painting the kind of picture which modern Academicians, when they wish to excuse a little cubism, are apt to call " Spirit Paintings." But, as it was, he did not always allow himself enough freedom. It was extremely fortunate – it would hardly be reasonable to attribute it to the cunning of so irrational a being as Blake – that he discovered for the illumination of his writings a process which allowed him great freedom of line. And it is in these etched illuminations that one can most appreciate its grace and vitality.

An extraordinary opulence and luxury often invest his line, even when he is describing the purest lily, the most child-like being. And there seems to be a kind of vegetable freedom in his designs ; they have the vitality, the spontaneous growth, of a natural object. Here the medium does not allow him to dwell on the muscles of the human body, and it is impossible to define any form very sharply or to describe it in any great detail. Thus his figures stand as if they had just sprung from the soil, or droop with a voluptuous exhaustion like tropical flowers. And everywhere there are tendrils which coil about his figures as if they were the stems from which these have grown. The vegetable universe is, in fact, triumphant, and the profusion of its growth is sometimes so sinister that one can hardly be surprised that Blake was afraid of it and, where he could, suppressed it by using pure outline and the classical canon of the human figure. His serpents, persons under the rule of reason, and other monsters are far more appalling in this dis- guise of vegetable exuberance than when they are merely classical or Michelangelesque embodiments of pity and terror. Nebuchadnezzar, one of the saddest cases of submission to reason which ever came to Blake's notice, is the more awful because he seems to be slowly changing into the grass which he eats.

These illuminations are, of course, decorative in intention, and the complexities of design which we look for in an easel picture are seldom to be found in them. But the disposition of these com- paratively simple shapes is often so perfect that we should expect to find Blake well able to de- sign on a larger scale and in a more elaborate manner. And yet it is seldom that he was able to do so. In his large engraving of the Canter- bury Pilgrims, a work with which he took immense trouble, the figures go straight across the picture

plane in a very mechanical way. Most of his
larger compositions are, it is true, more interesting,
but whenever Blake had to dispose a large number
of figures – even when these figures are not tightly
drawn with a classical formula – they are apt to
be connected by rather too emphatic and obvious
rhythms. " The Spiritual form of Nelson guiding
Leviathan," a painting in tempera which is now
in the Tate Gallery, is a very fair example of his
more elaborate compositions, but such an arrange-
ment of many figures is hardly suitable for the
flat design, with barely a hint of the third dimen-
sion, which Blake almost always produced. Yet
tempera seems to have been the medium most
suitable for Blake's talents, at any rate in his
larger works. Like his method of illumination,
tempera, even though he himself said that " all
Frescoes are as high in finish as miniatures or
enamels," did not allow him to draw with any
hard precision or to give a tight description of
every detail. And thus, almost as if against his
will, he had to employ his peculiar sensibility.
The little picture of Bathsheba, which is also in
the Tate Gallery, is an exquisite design in which,
for once, both the medium and the subject are
exactly suited to his sensibility. What he had to
do here was neither above nor below his powers ;
it was precisely suited to bring them out. Just so

much illusion of space as he could compass is here ; the few figures are described with no more precision than is necessary for the free and exquisite grace of his line, and the vegetation and landscape are simple enough for Blake to be able to express in them his peculiar languid and yet vital rhythms.

Towards the end of his life Blake seems to have grown more aware that a free handling, a swift and unrestricted calligraphy, was necessary for the expression of his sensibility. His celebrated engravings to illustrate the Book of Job are far more free in their rhythms, and the figures are far less tightly drawn than in the earlier engravings. But, even so, it seems to me that these engravings are sometimes too tight and hard, and some of the designs are too complicated for him to work out without growing mechanical. He still needed the help of a more congenial medium. Thus his woodcut illustrations for Thornton's *Virgil*, a medium in which he was inexperienced, are far fresher and more subtle, and this in spite of the fact that Blake profoundly disapproved of the book. " I look upon this," he wrote on the title page of his copy, " as a Most Malignant & Artful attack upon the Kingdom of Jesus By the Classical Learned thro' the instrumentality of Dr. Thornton. The Greek & Roman Classics is the Antichrist."

GB

It is interesting to see that Blake's powers of imaginative illustration suffer almost as much as the quality of his line from his taste for the rigid definition of every form. These minute woodcuts are in many ways more romantic and essentially poetical than the far more elaborate engravings of the Book of Job. The first conception of the engravings is often magnificent, but the details become sterile when they are worked out and given a precise form. In the woodcuts there is no room and no need for such precision, and Blake can inhabit his remote universe without filling it with tediously classical furniture. It is extraordinary with how little material these slight woodcuts suggest a distant, visionary world, a lunar landscape. There are no obvious symbols of eternity, no violent flights of the imagination. The effect seems to be produced in the main by Blake's use of chiaroscuro, but it is not, of course, the chiaroscuro of our own vegetable universe. Like the Byzantines, Blake could use an arbitrary light and shade, which, as it happens, is very easily obtained in a woodcut, in such a way as to surround every object with a rarefied, visionary atmosphere. " In expressing conditions of glaring and flickering light," Ruskin said, " Blake is greater than Rembrandt," a remark which would have seemed insulting to Blake and is insulting to Rembrandt. But it is perfectly true that Blake's singular use of chiaroscuro is often an important element in his most imaginative illustrations.

Certainly their unearthly lighting, sometimes infinitely sinister, sometimes benign, but always fantastic, is of great significance in the series of water-colours to illustrate Dante, on which Blake was at work just before his death. Many of these are now hung in the Tate Gallery, and they are often considered the finest of his water-colours. And here he has almost entirely conquered the repressive effect of outline. He is still rather better at foliage and monsters, which are here drawn with a marvellous spontaneity, than at the human figure, but the figures never interrupt the design with any too mechanical forms. Blake always had an astonishing fertility in invention, but we often have to recognise this faculty in the same way as we recognise the invention of an artist in an engraving made after his work. It has been remarked that Blake's pictures are apt to seem better in remembrance than when we are actually confronted with them, because in memory we only think of the scheme and design, not the details with which the first scheme is supported. But in the Dante illustrations even the details are exquisite and Blake allows himself

to use the monstrous paint-brush with great
freedom.    The blotting and blurring demons
appear to have been particularly active, and the
result is admirable.

# CHAPTER V

Blake's three years at Felpham – William Hayley – trial for treason – discontent – return to London – Malkin's memoir of his son – quarrel with Cromek – epigrams on Hayley – the exhibition of 1809.

DURING the seven years which he spent at Lambeth, Blake had worked incessantly for his living and had been engaged in a fierce struggle with all his conflicting emotions. The strain must have been appalling, and it is easy to understand the enthusiasm with which, in the year 1800, he welcomed the prospect of a holiday. Flaxman had introduced him to that writer of indifferent verses, William Hayley, the author of *The Triumphs of Temper*, " for ever feeble," as Byron described him, " and for ever tame." Unaware of the peculiar unsuitability of Blake as a companion for a mild writer of sentimental verses, Hayley probably thought that an uneducated engraver with a taste for poetry – Flaxman had some time before sent to Hayley a copy of the *Poetical Sketches* with an apologetic letter about the poet's defective education – would make a sympathetic and submissive illustrator of his books. After trying him with one or two small jobs, Hayley suggested that Blake should come and live near him at Felpham, a pleasant seaside place in Sussex, and make a set of engravings for Hayley's life of Cowper.

Blake was enchanted, but it was not enough for him to express a simple delight in the prospect of a seaside holiday. " The time is arrived," he at once concluded," when men shall again converse in Heaven and walk with angels." And Mrs. Blake wrote with equal excitement to Mrs. Flaxman – I am afraid that one must conclude that Blake helped her with the letter, though it would be pleasant to think that she could on occasion write exactly like her husband – " The swallows call us, fleeting past our window at this moment. Oh ! how we delight in talking of the pleasure we shall have in preparing you a summer bower at Felpham. And we not only talk, but behold ! the angels of our journey have inspired a song to you." And there follows a poem by Blake :

*Away to sweet Felpham, for Heaven is there ;*
*The Ladder of Angels descends through the air ;*
*On the Turret its spiral does softly descend,*
*Through the village then winds, at my cot it does end.*

*You stand in the village and look up to Heaven ;*
*And precious stones glitter on flights seventy-seven ;*
*And my brother is there, and my Friend and Thine,*
*Descend and ascend with the Bread and the Wine.*

*The Bread of sweet thought and the Wine of delight*
*Feed the village of Felpham by day and by night ;*
*And at his own door the bless'd hermit does stand,*
*Dispensing, unceasing, to all the wide land.*

The hermit is Hayley himself, who often liked to call himself, and to be called, the hermit of Eartham, where he had previously lived.

Nor was Blake disappointed when he arrived at Felpham, which was at once seen to be " more spiritual than London." " Heaven opens here on all sides her golden gates ; her windows are not obstructed by vapours ; voices of celestial inhabitants are most distinctly heard, and their forms more distinctly seen ; and my cottage is also a shadow of their houses." For his cottage also was transfigured. " It is a perfect model for Cottages &, I think, for Palaces of Magnificence, only Enlarging, not altering its proportions, and adding ornaments and not principles. Nothing can be more grand than its simplicity and usefulness ! " Here he was to live " a new life," and his new happiness was evidently a sign of the recognition of his merits in heaven, for " I am more famed in Heaven for my works than I could well conceive. In my brain are studies and chambers filled with books and pictures of old, which I wrote and painted in ages of eternity before my mortal life ;

and those works are the delight and study of
Archangels." Finally there was a significant and
beautiful omen of felicity. He met a plough on the
first morning after his arrival, and the ploughboy
said to the ploughman, "Father, the gate is open."
And so " I have begun to work, and find that I
can work with greater pleasure than ever." He at
once began to decorate Hayley's new library with
the heads of eighteen personages, among whom
were Hayley's illegitimate son, and " the poets
Milton, Homer, Camoens, Ercilla, Ariosto, and
Spenser, whose physiognomies have been my
delightful study." Hayley taught Blake to paint
miniatures, at which art Blake grew surprisingly
proficient, although, as he himself said, " portrait
painting is the direct contrary to designing and
historical painting, in every respect. If you have
not nature before you for every touch, you cannot
paint portrait ; and if you have nature before you
at all, you cannot paint history. It was Michael
Angelo's opinion and is mine." He also decorated
with wood-engravings a ballad by Hayley, which
was printed and sold for a charitable purpose, with
the title *Little Tom the Sailor*. It is perhaps worth
quoting a few lines, if only to show what the
*Songs of Innocence* would have been like if Blake had
not been supremely gifted as a lyrical poet.

*And does then the Ocean possess*
*The promising brave, little youth,*
*Who display'd, in a scene of distress,*
*Such Tenderness, Courage, and Truth ?*

*Little Tom is a Cottager's Son ;*
*His years not amounting to ten !*
*But the Dawn of his Manhood begun*
*With a soul like the noblest of Men.*

*In a Hospital distant from Home,*
*He lost his unfortunate Sire ;*
*And his Mother was tempted to roam,*
*But to see that kind Father expire.*

Yet for the moment Blake even thought Hayley's
verses, the verses which Felpham " produces by
her eldest son," better than his own. In short,
" Mr. Hayley acts like a prince. I am at complete
ease."

But, alas, both Hayley and the archangels
seemed determined to disappoint him. After a
year Blake wrote in evident distress to his patron,
Thomas Butts, and his reaction to his discomfort is
extremely interesting. He had allowed himself to
be carried away by the exquisite enthusiasm which
at first transfigured all Felpham, a spontaneous
outburst of joy like that of the *Songs of Innocence*

or of the visions of his childhood. But later, when he was disappointed, he began to be afraid of his fantasies and even, it would seem, to seek a refuge in " the world of duty and reality," to fly from his miseries not away from but towards reality :

" I accomplish not one half of what I intend, because my abstract folly hurries me often away while I am at work, carrying me over mountains and valleys, which are not real, into a land of abstraction where spectres of the dead wander. This I endeavour to prevent ; I, with my whole might, chain my feet to the world of duty and reality. But in vain ! the faster I bind, the better is the ballast ; for I, so far from being bound down, take the world with me in my flights, and often it seems lighter than a ball of wool rolled by the wind."

He even thought, it would seem, of calling upon the materialists Bacon and Newton to help him back to reality. " Bacon and Newton would prescribe ways of making the world heavier to me . . ." And he continues : " Alas ! wretched, happy, ineffectual labourer of Time's moments that I am ! who shall deliver me from this spirit of abstraction and improvidence ? " But in this extraordinary moment of insight which disappointment brought to him, he still saw that the hope cf chaining himself to reality was vain, that the help of Bacon and Newton was not for him.

It was inevitable that Felpham should not come up to his expectations, but his misfortunes were worse than he could have expected. In the damp cottage which he had taken both he and Mrs. Blake suffered from rheumatism – Mrs. Blake was seriously ill – and, extraordinary as it may seem, Blake was prosecuted for high treason. A certain private soldier, Scholfield by name (he appears in the prophetic books as Skofeld, and, inevitably, as a most sinister figure), was found digging in Blake's garden, and Blake turned him out. Without Blake's knowledge, he had been invited to help the gardener who was working there. As before, when he had seen the boy with a log tied to his leg, Blake did not hesitate.

" I desired him, as politely as possible, to go out of the garden ; he refused. I still persisted in desiring his departure. He then threatened to knock out my eyes, with many abominable imprecations, and with some contempt for my person ; it affronted my foolish pride. I therefore took him by the elbows, and pushed him before me till I had got him out.  There I intended to have left him, but he, turning about, put himself into a posture of defiance, threatening and swearing at me.  I, perhaps foolishly and perhaps not, stepped out at the gate, and, putting aside his blows, took him again by the elbows, and, keeping his back to me, pushed him forward down the road about fifty yards – he all the while endeavouring to turn round and strike me, and raging and cursing, which drew out several neighbours."

It was very fortunate that the neighbours arrived; not only did they constrain Scholfield, but they were able to act as witnesses for Blake's defence.  For Scholfield promptly took out a warrant against Blake for assault and seditious words, and accused him of saying, as Blake discreetly puts it, " D—— the K——."  Although he was able to give so clear and sensible an account of the matter, Blake was evidently inclined to generalise his trouble, to see in it only one example of the persistent persecution of fate.  In the same letter, describing the incident to Thomas Butts, he was moved to include a poem in which he used of himself almost the same words which he had put into the mouth of Mary – perhaps of Mary Wollestonecraft :

*O why was I born with a different face ?*
*Why was I not born like the rest of my race ?*
*When I look, each one starts ; when I speak, I offend ;*
*Then I'm silent and passive, & lose every friend.*

But though he had begun to see more in the incident than met the eye, and was later to include it as an integral part of his imaginary universe, this in no way affected his conduct. At the trial he defended himself with spirit and ability. It is said that, when the soldier gave his evidence, Blake cried out " False ! " in so impressive a manner that the whole court was thrilled and convinced. His notes for his defence, probably written for the use of his counsel, have survived, and it is curious to see that Blake seizes upon a point with the skill of a practised lawyer. What could be more ingenious and convincing than this argument ?

" The soldier has been heard to say repeatedly that he did not know how the Quarrel began, which he would not say if such seditious words were spoken."

And after arranging with great precision the evidence in his favour, he concludes with this excellent and cogent appeal.

" If such Perjury as this can take effect, any Villain in future may come and drag me and my

Wife out of our House, and beat us in the Garden
or use us as he please or is able, and afterwards
go and swear our Lives away.

" Is it not in the Power of any Thief who enters
a Man's Dwelling and robs him, or misuses his
Wife or Children, to go and swear as this Man
has sworn ? "

The case was heard at length and Blake was
acquitted.  He had excited so much sympathy
among the public who had come to hear the case
that "in defiance," as the *Sussex Advertiser* considered, " of all decency," he was loudly cheered
when the verdict was given.

It may seem a trivial and absurd affair, but Blake
was in real danger.  It was a time when it was
even more dangerous to be thought a French spy
or a Jacobin than it was to be thought a German
spy during the last war, and the country was in
the same state of suspicion.  Coleridge was very
nearly arrested for talking about Spinoza, a word
which contains the dangerous syllable " spy."
Moreover, Blake's revolutionary past might well
have been remembered against him, though by
good fortune it was not.

But Hayley himself was a worse nuisance.  He
had his own ideas both about poetry and engraving.  He made imbecile suggestions, he read

Klopstock aloud, until Blake's heart knocked
against the root of his tongue. For his life of
Cowper Hayley wanted " a device of *the Bible
upright* supporting *The Task*, with a laurel leaf and
*Palms* . . . neatly copied by our kind Blake." For
*The Elephant : A Series of Ballads*, he wanted a
variety of animals. He asked to see the prophetic
book which Blake had in hand, and then " looked
with sufficient contempt to enhance my opinion
of it." Blake was never allowed to do what he
wanted. " I find on all hands great objection to
my doing anything but the mere drudgery of
business." But here he was firm, and neither
would nor could make any concessions. " I too
well remember the threats I heard ! " – the threats
of angels who warned him, " If you, who are
organised for spiritual communion, refuse, and
bury your talent in the earth, even though you
should want natural bread, sorrow and despera-
tion pursue you through life, and after death
shame and confusion of face to eternity. Everyone
in eternity will leave you, aghast at the man who
was crowned with glory and honour by his
brethren, and betrayed their cause to their
enemies. You will be called the base Judas who
betrayed his friend ! " Blake withdrew for comfort
to his own opinion of himself, writing to Thomas
Butts, to whom it was a relief to pour out all his

troubles with the knowledge that they would be amiably received, in a strain which wavered between the superb and the ridiculous, between natural pride and megalomania. " Be assured, dear friend," he says at one moment, " that there is not one touch in those drawings and pictures but what came from my head and my heart in unison," yet at another moment he cannot help boasting, " There is nothing in the art which our painters do that I can confess myself ignorant of. I also know and understand, and can assuredly affirm, that the works I have done for you are equal to the Caracci or Raphael. . . ." And of the prophetic book which he was writing, the *Milton*, " I consider it the grandest poem that this world contains." For a while, it would seem, Blake even succeeded in impressing Hayley by such assertions. " Indeed, by my late firmness I have brought down his affected loftiness, and he begins to think that I have some genius ; as if genius and assurance were the same thing ! " For the moment he was victorious, and he could write in triumph : " Nothing can withstand the fury of my Course among the Stars of God & in the Abysses of the Accuser." But, in the end, Hayley had no difficulty in withstanding the fury of Blake's course. His " Genteel Ignorance & Polite Disapprobation " – it is remarkable how precisely and wittily

Blake could describe the less spiritual of his annoyances – proved too strong. They quarrelled, made it up again, quarrelled again, and it was finally agreed in a more or less friendly way that Blake should return to London " with the full approbation of Mr. Hayley."

Once again Blake had been deceived, and after so much expectation and enthusiasm he could only conclude that " the Visions were angry with me at Felpham." But he did not, as at the beginning of his disappointment, attempt to flee from them. On the contrary, the involved conflict between Blake and Hayley was reflected, in the prophetic book *Milton*, as a yet more involved conflict between supernatural beings. Blake's observation of Hayley's character enabled him to add new subleties to the character of Satan and to discover new modes of deception in the father of lies. The most dangerous, the really paralysing weapon which Satan now used against the spirits of prophecy and poetry was an " incomparable mildness " which he must have learnt from Hayley. And when Satan was heard –

*Himself exculpating with mildest speech, for himself believ'd*
*That he had not oppress'd nor injur'd the refractory servants –*

HB

it was almost impossible to circumvent such elaborate self-deception, or for the poet to avoid serving in " the Mills of Satan."

But the thought of returning to London at once cheered him, and " I can alone," Blake wrote while still at Felpham, " carry on my visionary studies in London unannoyed." There alone, " I may converse with my friends in eternity, see visions, dream dreams, and prophecy and speak parables unobserved, and at liberty from the doubts of other mortals." And, once returned to London, he found there a new though soberer paradise. " The shops in London improve . . . and the streets are widened where they were narrow." Mrs. Blake recovered from her rheumatism – " Electricity is the wonderful cause," – and Blake even began to feel some compunction for his treatment of Hayley – he speaks of " the pang of affection and gratitude " – and wrote him many enthusiastic letters of thanks. In fact, he was now so happy, and had apparently forgotten so completely the trials which disturbed his " three years' slumber on the banks of the ocean," that he could write, " O lovely Felpham, parent of immortal friendship, to thee I am eternally indebted for my three years' rest from perturbation and the strength I now enjoy." He thought no more of taking refuge in reality or in the heavy

reason of Newton. On the contrary, the spectre
of reason was now finally conquered :

" For now ! O Glory ! and O delight ! I have
entirely reduced that spectrous fiend to his station,
whose annoyance has been the ruin of my labours
for the last passed twenty years of my life. He
is the enemy of conjugal love, and is the Jupiter
of the Greeks, an iron-hearted tyrant, the ruiner
of Ancient Greece. I speak with perfect confidence and certainty of the fact which has passed
upon me. Nebuchadnezzar had seven times
passed over him ; I have had twenty. Thank God
I was not altogether a beast as he was ; but I was
a slave bound in a mill among beasts and devils.
These beasts and these devils are now, together
with myself, become children of light and liberty,
and my feet and my wife's feet are free from
fetters."

Moreover, during the last twenty years his rigid
but not quite bestial submission to reason had, as
he suddenly saw, been the cause of his comparative failure in painting :

" Everyone of my friends was astonished at my
faults, and could not assign a reason ; they knew
my industry and abstinence from every pleasure

for the sake of study, and yet – and yet – and yet
there wanted the proofs of industry in my works."

Blake was willing to reject the past, and those
works which once were the equal of Raphael, for
the sake of the future.  For now everything was to
be altered.  He had been to see a collection of old
masters, an experience for which he had always
longed.  Had it not been one of the delights of
Felpham that it was almost as near to Paris,
where there are so many works of art, as to London ?  It is true that this collection contained
many forgeries and was, in the opinion of Lawrence, almost worthless, but this made no
difference to Blake.  On seeing them " I was again
enlightened with the light I enjoyed in my youth
and which has for exactly twenty years been closed
from me as by a door and by window shutters. . . .
Dear Sir," he continues, writing to Hayley,
" excuse my enthusiasm or rather madness, for I am
really drunk with intellectual vision whenever I
take a pencil or graver into my hand, even as I
used to be in my youth, and as I have not been
for twenty dark, but very profitable years. . . .
In a short time I shall make good my assertion
that I am become suddenly as I was."

But the illumination, once again, hardly lasted.
London, he had already found, was " a city of

assassinations." At first he set to work engraving
with enthusiasm. He was still employed by
Hayley and was illustrating a life of Romney, a
painter for whom he had what must now seem to
us a rather irresponsible admiration. And he was
introduced by the engraver Cromek to Dr.
Benjamin Heath Malkin, headmaster of Bury
Grammar School. Malkin wrote a memoir of his
son, who had died in his seventh year, already
" an expert linguist, a general reader, something
of a poet," and most skilful in copying engravings
after Raphael. And, what must have been of
particular interest to Blake, the child had already
begun to invent an imaginary universe ; he had,
at any rate, made a map of an imaginary country
of which he also wrote the history. Blake was
employed to make an engraving from a miniature
of the child at the age of two, and to surround it
with an emblematic design. He was also asked to
write an appreciation of the child's drawings, in
which he found " firm determinate outline." And
he continued, with a vigorous but singularly inappropriate attack on the opposite school of
painting – " had the hand which executed these
little ideas been that of a plagiary, who works
only from the memory, we should have seen blots,
called masses . . . blots without form and therefore
without meaning." With the map, as we should

expect, he was delighted, and he found in it " the same character of the firm and determinate." In fact he saw that the child was already proceeding in precisely the same path which he had marked out for himself. " All his efforts," he wrote, " prove this little boy to have had that greatest of blessings, a strong imagination, a clear idea, and a determinate vision of things in his own mind."

Cromek, for some reason, re-engraved Blake's frontispiece for this book, but he soon did worse. He proposed that Blake should both design and engrave illustrations for Blair's poem " The Grave." But Cromek only purchased twelve instead of twenty of Blake's designs and, breaking his contract, handed them over to another engraver, Schiavonetti. It was a bitter disappointment, not made easier to bear by Cromek's rudeness, for Blake had hoped that at last he would appeal through this work to a larger public. And Blake's friends were as tactless as Cromek was rude. Flaxman and Stothard apparently suggested that Blake's designs were improved by Schiavonetti's engraving, an opinion which Blake compared, in one of his peculiarly vicious epigrams, to Hayley's opinion that Pope improved Homer. For in the midst of these disasters Blake began to remember once more how much he had

suffered from Hayley. They were still correspond-
ing, and still exchanging elaborate compliments,
but Blake began to tire. He called Hayley " The
Pick Thank," and wrote in his note-book this
epigram :

> *I write the Rascal Thanks till he & I*
> *With Thanks & Compliments are quite drawn dry.*

He began to remember " Felpham's old mill,"
which he had used as the model for the mill of
Satan. His rage increased, and Hayley was
annihilated in two more lines :

> *Of H[ayley]'s birth this was the happy lot,*
> *His Mother on his Father him begot.*

Finally his anger, his sense of injury, passed all
bounds. This mild and genial country squire, who
had so amiably taken to the encouragement of the
arts, became a monster worse than the Satan of
the prophetic books.

> *When H[ayley] finds out what you cannot do,*
> *That is the very thing he'll set you to.*
> *If you break not your Neck, 'tis not his fault,*
> *But pecks of poison are not pecks of salt.*
> *And when he could not act upon my wife*
> *Hired a Villain to bereave my Life.*

It is a pity that none of the letters have survived which at this time, as he seems to suggest, he was writing to Hayley. It would have been interesting to read the compliments and thanks which Hayley managed to extract from Blake at the very time when he was revolving in his mind these dark suspicions.

Whatever Blake may have suspected of his enemies was confirmed by Cromek's further persecutions. For Cromek, or so Blake thought – for it is difficult to be certain of the rights and wrongs of the matter – was entirely without scruples. Having seen a drawing by Blake of the Canterbury Pilgrims, presumably made as a design for an engraving, he stole the idea and commissioned a picture of the same subject from Stothard. Blake was furious and wretched, and the fragile equilibrium of his mind was still further disturbed. He projected a public address on the subject of the Canterbury Pilgrims which is full of bitterness and rage, of wild assertions and complaints that everyone's hand was against him. Inevitably, it contains an epigram on Hayley. And yet in the prospectus for his own engraving of the Canterbury Pilgrims he was able to compose an admirable criticism and appreciation of Chaucer's characters, though his chief intention was to show how incompetently his rival had understood

Chaucer. His distemper could make him write
nonsense and hysterical abuse, but it could not
prevent him, when he was not writing of some
point that touched on his delusions, from using
his intuition and his intellect. And it did not
prevent him, as perhaps quotations from his
letters have shown, from writing magnificent
prose.

For the first time Blake had met not only with
neglect, but, as it seemed to him, with positive
hostility, and not only in the spiritual sphere, but
from actual human beings. Scholfield's absurd
malignity was nothing to this. He determined to
make his one final effort to show his works to the
public and to prove that he was a great artist.
And so, in 1809, he held an exhibition of his most
important pictures in the shop of his brother,
James Blake. On the advertisement of the exhibition he put the motto, " Fit audience find, tho'
few," and he composed an elaborate descriptive
catalogue in which there is much that is interesting, much that is obviously the work of a great
mind, but more that is absurd, wandering, provoc-
ative, and obviously inspired by his delusions.
And, alas, the audience, though few, seems to have
been unfit. At any rate, the exhibition did not
establish Blake's reputation, and, still worse, a
painful review was printed in the *Examiner* in

which he was described as " an unfortunate lunatic, whose personal inoffensiveness secures him from confinement," though why this should be a reason for attacking his pictures the art critic of the *Examiner* does not explain.

# CHAPTER VI

Years of neglect – " The Everlasting Gospel " – lost works –
friendship with Linnell – conversations with Crabb Robinson
– *The Ancients* – Blake's death.

FOR some years after these reverses Blake was
neglected, poor, and alone. There are few records
of this time, and a contemporary critic who wished
to meet Blake found in 1817 that " so entire is the
uncertainty, in which he is involved, that after
many enquiries, I meet with some in doubt
whether he is still in existence." But Southey had
seen him a year before, and later recorded that
" his madness was too evident – too fearful " for
it to be possible to take any pleasure in his company. And Blake himself paid a visit to the Rev.
Thomas Dibdin, apparently to ask him about
Milton, a poet about whom he had already
written a prophetic book. He had been asked by
Milton's spirit to correct certain errors in *Paradise
Lost*. Dibdin "soon found the amiable but illusory
Blake far beyond my ken or sight. In an instant
he is in his ' third heaven ' – flapped by the wings
of seraphs, such as his own genius only could
shape, and his pencil embody. The immediate
subject of our discussion – and for which indeed

he professed in some measure to have visited me –
was ' the minor poems of Milton.' Never were
such dreamings poured forth as were poured forth
by my original visitor ; – his stature mean, his
head big and round, his forehead broad and high,
his eyes blue, large and lambent. . . ."

But it was at this time that Blake was finishing
the most complicated and difficult of all his
prophetic books, *Jerusalem* : *The Emanation of the
Giant Albion*, which is, in the main, a statement
of his beliefs about the English and the Jews,
though these theories are inextricably involved
with his own mythology and his own philosophy.
And at the same time he composed a much shorter
poem, " The Everlasting Gospel," which only
exists in fragments of a rough draft. In it there
are several of those interludes of beauty of which
he was always capable when for the moment he
turned aside from the confusion of his delusional
universe. And the poem has a curious air of
finality ; it reads like the last conclusions of a man
who has been through endless and harassing sur-
mises. " Do what you will," he decides,

> *Do what you will this life's a fiction
> And is made up of Contradiction.*

It is like a final summary of all the effort so long
and so vainly expended in the prophetic books.

And most of the poem is beautifully lucid and a remarkable contrast to *Jerusalem*. Its statements have an extraordinary force and decision, and it is the most perfect statement of Blake's religion, as opposed to his mythology, his mysticism, or whatever it may be called. Moral virtues, he argues, are nothing to do with religion, and even Christ did not preach or practise them ; forgiveness is everything, and the Christian religion differs from all others because it preaches forgiveness of sins. It is not precisely the accepted doctrine of Christianity, but it might well have proved a haven for Blake. One can hardly doubt that about this time he was in a mood of resignation, inclined to seek the substantial emotion behind the elaborate constructions of his troubled mind. Thus he turned to his earlier poem, " The Gates of Paradise," perhaps the most mysterious but also the most beautiful product of his earlier mysticism, and added an epilogue. This, it is true, is addressed to " The Accuser who is the God of this World," for by now God and the Devil were inextricably combined in his mind, both by confusion of substance and by unity of person. But the second verse of the epilogue expresses at once an almost weary scepticism and a passionate faith in the final remnant of religious emotion which is left.

*Tho' thou art Worship'd by the Names Divine*
*Of Jesus & Jehovah, thou art still*
*The Son of Morn in weary Night's decline,*
*The lost Traveller's Dream under the Hill.*

We might judge that Blake had somehow come to terms with his mind and had at last found a final state of equilibrium, if there were not later works and records of his conversation to show that he returned to his former preoccupations.

He continued, even when most neglected, to write with the same prodigious energy and as copiously as ever. Indeed, at the end of his life he told Crabb Robinson that he had written "more than Voltaire or Rousseau – six or seven epic poems as long as Homer, and twenty tragedies as long as *Macbeth*." No tragedies remain, if indeed he ever wrote any beyond his first attempt at a Shakespearean play. But at this time he could not afford the expense of engraving his works. Scores of manuscripts were produced, which lay about and were lost or destroyed. It is known, for example, that Tatham burnt some of the most heretical of his manuscripts, and one of these lost works had the fascinating title *The Book of Moonlight*. There was also the *Vision of Genesis*, from which Blake read aloud to Robinson " a wild passage in a sort of Bible style." Another, *For Children : The*

*Gates of Hell*, is also lost, and if it was a comple-
mentary work to the poem *For Children : The Gates
of Paradise*, it is a more serious loss than the missing
prophetic books.   It is said that he made many
unsuccessful attempts to get his works published
in the ordinary way, and, after the inevitable
refusals, would say, " Well, it is published elsewhere, and " – here his engaging confidence in the
smallest details of the eternal world came to help
him – " beautifully bound."

But in 1818 he was rescued at least from poverty
and neglect.   He made the acquaintance of John
Linnell, already a successful artist though then
only twenty-six years of age.   Linnell gave him
many commissions, but he did more, he sincerely
admired his pictures, he treated his mythology with
the greatest respect, and he introduced him to a
number of young artists, who, so far from believing
him to be mad, thought him a prophet.   Among
these was the water-colourist John Varley, an
adept in astrology.   Linnell and Varley encouraged
Blake to make drawings of his visions, and there
is an extraordinary account of him drawing visionary beings exactly as if he had a model before
his eyes.   When he drew the ghost of a flea, for
example, he had to pause while the object opened
its mouth, make a drawing of the open mouth, and
then continue the original drawing when the sitter

shut its mouth. Since one knows how circum-
stantial an account of the supernatural or of a
*séance* may be, even when it is quite untrue, there
is no particular reason to believe that this is
exactly what happened, though there still exists a
most remarkable drawing of the flea's ghost both
with its mouth open and with its mouth shut.
According to Varley, while it was sitting " the Flea
told him that all fleas were inhabited by the souls
of such men as were by nature bloodthirsty to
excess, and were therefore providentially confined to the size and form of insects ; otherwise,
were he himself, for instance, the size of a
horse, he would depopulate a great portion of
the country."

Blake made about forty or fifty such visionary
drawings for Varley, among which were some
" Types of Insanity." He had been reading in
that year Spurzheim's *Observations on the Deranged
Manifestations of the Mind, or Insanity,* and seems to
have been much interested in them and to have
drawn from them the conclusion that he himself
was mad. For where Spurzheim says, speaking of
Methodism as a common cause of insanity, that
" the primitive feelings of religion may be misled
and produce insanity," Blake wrote in the margin –
it is a puzzling though important document of his
mind – " Cowper came to me and said ' O that I

were insane always. I will never rest. Can you not make me truly insane ? I will never rest till I am so. O that in the bosom of God I was hid.' " And Cowper continues – it must be held in mind that he is supposed to be speaking of Blake himself, " You retain health and yet are as mad as any of us all – over us all – mad as a refuge from unbelief – from Bacon, Newton and Locke." Among the visionary heads there was also " The Man who Built the Pyramids," a creature of almost bestial stupidity, weakly smiling, for Blake believed that the gods of Egypt were mathematical diagrams, and her architecture a symbol of crass materialism. It is interesting to see that many personages from English history appear among these visionary heads, which seems to suggest that Blake never lost that interest in the subject, as a possible field for apocalyptic revelation, which he had shown in his earliest works.

Linnell lived in Hampstead, and Blake used to visit his house and talk of the deepest subjects with Varley and his host. Varley believed that Blake's mythology could be given an astrological significance, that an obscure episode could be given a meaning if, for instance, it referred to " Sagittarius crossing Taurus." Linnell never contradicted Blake or showed any impatience or incredulity, but he would labour for long to find reason in his

Iʙ

sayings. " A stranger," Gilchrist says, " hearing
the three talk of spirits and astrology in this matter-
of-fact way, would have been mystified." Indeed,
the conversation, even to an intimate, must have
been sufficiently intricate. But Blake was happy
in this sympathetic company. He often made his
way to Hampstead, even though Hampstead and
all places north of London always laid him up the
day after he had visited them with the same complaint, " and the same torment of the stomach."
" Sir Francis Bacon would say, it is want of dis-
cipline in mountainous places. Sir Francis Bacon
is a liar."

At this time Crabb Robinson paid many visits
to Blake, and found him, in his old age, " pale,
with a Socratic countenance, and an expression of
great sweetness, but bordering on weakness –
except when his features are animated by expression, and then he has an air of inspiration about
him." They talked mostly of art and poetry, but
also of religion and philosophy, and Robinson was
evidently puzzled, sometimes shocked – he had to
conceal in German the fact that Blake believed
that the Bible recommended community of wives
– but often interested and admiring. He sometimes attempted to argue, against the supposition
that Dante and Wordsworth were atheists, against
the Manichæan heresy that the Devil was as

powerful as God, against Blake's conviction that evil did not exist, or that the world was flat. " I objected," Robinson says, " the circumnavigation." But no arguments, however cogent, could ruffle Blake or disturb his convictions. " I know what is true," he said, " by internal conviction. A doctrine is told me – my heart says it must be true." Indeed, his opinions were now so firmly fixed that he could listen patiently to Robinson, with " genuine dignity and independence," in the untroubled possession of his thoughts. He was quiet, self-possessed and modest, and when he spoke of his visions, " it was in the ordinary unemphatic tone in which we speak of trivial matters."

In such a tone, using " delicacy in his words," he told Robinson that he had committed many murders, that he saw the spiritual sun on Primrose Hill, that the Supreme Being was liable to error, and that Milton had warned him not to be misled by the mistakes in *Paradise Lost.* But "his eye glistened " when he spoke of the pleasures of art. The spirit had said to him, " Blake, be an artist and nothing else." " I should be sorry," he continued, " if I had any earthly fame, for whatever natural glory a man has is so much detracted from his spiritual glory. I wish to do nothing for profit. I wish to live for art. I want nothing whatever.

I am quite happy." He even tried to give to
Robinson the illuminated copies of his works which
Robinson wished to buy as a means of offering
charity. And so Robinson listened, determined
to draw Blake out, for he was obviously tired and
old, withdrawn into himself and in no mood for
argument, needing to be stirred by the mention of
some point of acute importance to him. But
Robinson was persistent with his prosaic enquiries,
assiduous even when shocked (he had but recently
wished his friends to cut Hazlitt for writing the
*Liber Amoris*) and he gathered excellent material
for his diary, only at intervals interrupting this
extraordinary conversation when he could bear it
no longer, when he was compelled to object the
circumnavigation. " It would be hard," he decided, " to give Blake's station between Christianity, Platonism, and Spinosism."

Blake was happier with the painters to whom
Linnell introduced him, and amongst them, at last,
he found disciples who were eager, young, and
attentive. He was old, but he opened himself to
them, and they listened, admired, and did not
provoke him. They had formed a premature Pre-
Raphaelite Brotherhood, calling themselves " The
Ancients " because they approved of nothing but
primitive art, and it seemed to them that they had
found a primitive in their midst. He was, thought

Samuel Palmer, who was a painter of romantic
landscapes and learnt much from Blake, " a fit
companion for Dante . . . his ideal home was with
Fra Angelico." It is true that Palmer, after
Blake's death, was troubled by the heterodoxy of
his writings, thinking that they " savoured of
Manichæism," as indeed they do. But to Linnell
himself Blake was " more like the ancient patterns
of virtue than I ever expected to see in this world,"
and to Tatham, who later wrote a brief life of
Blake, when they walked home together it was " as
if he were walking with the prophet Isaiah."
Richmond was a more matter-of-fact disciple ; he
would argue and contradict. Indeed, one would
hardly have expected to find him amongst this
group of advanced and enthusiastic artists. He
later married and had fifteen children, whom
he supported by doing for the Victorian age
what Sargent did for the Edwardians, and with
the same mechanical efficiency. But Blake
was very good-humoured with him, and he remained always in Richmond's mind as the most
disinterested and single-minded artist he had
known. To Finch, who was a painter in water-
colours and a Swedenborgian, Blake seemed " a
new kind of man." Edward Calvert, the most
original artist amongst them, learnt from Blake
that style which he developed in his idylls, a series

of engravings which are among the few triumphs of English illustration in the nineteenth century. And there was even a stockbroker in the company, a character about whom one would like to know more, who enjoyed a profound dislike of modern painting – " wretched work, Sir. . . . No room to get a thought in edgeways." He spoke of " the Divine Blake," who " had seen God, Sir, and talked with angels." The Ancients called Blake's rooms in Fountain Court " The House of the Interpreter," although, if there was one thing which Blake did not do, it was interpretation. In fact, with these young disciples and Blake as their prophet a new religion might well have begun had they not been painters, and unsuited to the work of conversion and organisation.

Blake enjoyed many pastoral expeditions with the Ancients, who were accustomed to meet at Shoreham and there paint in company. They wandered about the country by night as well as by day, wearing curious clothes and reciting poetry. The villagers of Shoreham called them, mysteriously, " The Extollagers." With Palmer and Calvert, Blake went by night to a haunted castle, where the ghost was discovered to be a snail. And Blake was able once again to exercise his powers of divination. Palmer had left the company to go to London, but, an hour after he had gone, Blake lifted his hand to his forehead and said, " Palmer is coming ; he is walking up the road." The others would not believe him, but in a minute Palmer walked in, the coach which was taking him to London having broken down. At moments Blake would still flash out with indignation, and would say, when he was prevented from working, that " he was being devoured by jackals and hyenas." And any talk of scientific matters he could not tolerate, interrupting such a conversation to say, " It is false, I walked the other evening to the end of the earth, and touched the sky with my fingers."

He still withdrew into himself at times, and, writing to Linnell, confessed to "intellectual peculiarity, that must be myself alone shut up in myself, or reduced to nothing." Nowhere is the force of Blake's intellect more apparent than in his descriptions of his own state of mind, so much more exact and to the point than anything which others have said about him. But for the most part he would talk willingly to the company, who would ask his advice and remember his sayings. Richmond, when he wondered if his powers of invention were failing, went at once to ask Blake's advice. Blake turned to his wife and said, " It is just so with us, is it not, for weeks together, when the visions forsake us ? What do we do then, Kate ? "

"We kneel down and pray, Mr. Blake." He no longer spoke in a tired, matter-of-fact voice but talked eagerly of his visionary experiences, expounded his philosophy, and told the young men how an artist should live. They listened and were converted.

But he was now growing weaker and failing in health, though not in mind. "I have been very near the gates of death," he wrote, "and have returned very weak and an old man, feeble and tottering, but not in spirit and life, not in the real man, the imagination, which liveth for ever. In that I am stronger and stronger, as this foolish body decays." He lay in his bed, from which he could look out of the window and see the Thames, and worked with unabated energy at the illustrations to Dante which Linnell had commissioned from him. A few days before his death, when he had finished colouring an etching, he turned to his wife, and said, "Stay, keep as you are, *you* have ever been an *angel* to me, I will draw you." He died singing, and saying of his songs, to his wife, "My beloved, they are not mine – no – they are not mine." He had no fear of death, to which and to heaven he had long looked forward. But his wife had already said of him, "I have very little of his company, he is always in paradise." And what little can be learnt from his writings about the remote world which Blake inhabited, must suggest the unexpected, almost disturbing conclusion that it was often paradise.  One might so easily have expected it to be, what it un-doubtedly was at times, the exact opposite.

# BIBLIOGRAPHY

*Poetry and Prose of William Blake*, edited by Geoffrey Keynes. Complete in one volume. The Nonesuch Press, 1927.

*The Life of William Blake*, by Mona Wilson. The Nonesuch Press, 1927. A new and cheaper edition, 1932.
This is the most complete and thorough life; it contains all the available facts and is a scholarly and admirable work.

*The Life of William Blake*, by Alexander Gilchrist. Edited, with an introduction, by W. Graham Robertson. John Lane, 1907.
A pleasant, discursive, and conversational biography. Gilchrist was able to consult many who actually knew or met Blake.

*William Blake*, by Arthur Symons. Constable, 1907.
In addition to his own life and criticism of Blake, Mr. Symons prints nearly all the allusions to, or accounts of, Blake by his contemporaries. These include Tatham's life, Allan Cunningham's life, J. T. Smith's biographical sketch, extracts from Crabb Robinson's diary, and various less important contemporary sources for his life.

*The Letters of William Blake.* Together with a life by Frederick Tatham. Edited, with an introduction and notes, by Archibald G. B. Russell. Methuen, 1906.

*D. G. Rossetti's Collected Works*, in two volumes. Ellis & Elvey, 1888. Contains Rossetti's criticism and appreciation of Blake.

*William Blake : A Critical Essay*, by Algernon Charles Swinburne. A new edition. Chatto & Windus, 1906.

*William Blake : His Philosophy and Symbols*, by S. Foster Damon. Constable, 1924.
An attempt to interpret the prophetic books and other works.

*Blake's Innocence and Experience : A Study of the Songs and Manuscripts, showing the two Contrary States of the Human Soul*, by Joseph H. Wicksteed, M.A. Dent, 1928.

*Blake and Modern Thought*, by Denis Saurat. Constable, 1929.

*William Blake*, by Basil de Selincourt. Duckworth, 1909.
Mr. Selincourt is mainly, though not exclusively, occupied with Blake's paintings and engravings.

*William Blake*. Vol. I. Illustrations of the Book of Job, with a general introduction by Laurence Binyon. Methuen, 1906.

*Books and Characters : French and English*, by Lytton Strachey. Chatto & Windus, 1922.
Contains an essay on the poetry of William Blake.

This list is not, of course, intended to be complete.